Social Issues
in Literature

Tyranny in
William Shakespeare's
Julius Caesar

Other Books in the Social Issues in Literature Series:

Social Issues
in Literature

Tyranny in
William Shakespeare's
Julius Caesar

Vernon Elso Johnson, Book Editor

GREENHAVEN PRESS
A part of Gale, Cengage Learning

Detroit • New York • San Francisco • New Haven, Conn • Waterville, Maine • London

Christine Nasso, *Publisher*
Elizabeth Des Chenes, *Managing Editor*

© 2011 Greenhaven Press, a part of Gale, Cengage Learning

LIBRARY OF CONGRESS CATALOGING-IN-PUBLICATION DATA

Tyranny in William Shakespeare's Julius Caesar / Vernon Elso Johnson, book editor.
    p. cm. -- (Social issues in literature)
    Includes bibliographical references and index.
    ISBN 978-0-7377-5262-5 -- ISBN 978-0-7377-5263-2 (pbk.)
  1. Shakespeare, William, 1564-1616. Julius Caesar. 2. Caesar, Julius--In literature. 3. Despotism in literature. I. Johnson, Vernon E. (Vernon Elso), 1921-
  PR2808.T96 2011
  822.3'3--dc22

                                             2010033610

Printed in the United States of America
2 3 4 5 6 7 15 14 13 12 11

Contents

Rather than sympathizing with one heroic figure, Shakespeare dramatizes the tragedy of the Roman Republic.

Brutus's noble revolution for the people is only an act; he is no more a true hero than Caesar is.

Chapter 3: Contemporary Perspectives on Tyranny

Introduction

In 1599 the first Globe Theatre opened in the neighborhood of Bankside on the River Thames outside London. It is believed that the Globe's premiere performance was the never-before-seen *Julius Caesar* by William Shakespeare. The theater burned down in 1613 during the performance of another Shakespeare play, *Henry VIII*. It was rebuilt in 1614 and then closed in 1642, when the Puritans closed all theaters. Then in 1999 *Julius Caesar* appeared again at the Globe (which had been reconstructed in 1997)—echoing as nearly as possible the original production. Meanwhile, throughout the four-century interval, critics, producers, and a wide reading audience have analyzed the play, disagreeing sometimes dramatically as to its basic meaning.

In the creation of *Julius Caesar*, Shakespeare departed from his usual practice and set this puzzling drama in ancient Rome, even as England struggled through an uncertain time for the monarchy and dominant aristocrats. The playwright shows the last days of Caesar's life after he has achieved absolute power as dictator for life; his murder by a group of aristocrats led by Cassius and Brutus, who hope to restore the Roman Republic; and the fatal aftermath of the conspirators' actions. Elizabethan audiences would have been familiar with the resulting crises and civil war that characterize many of Shakespeare's English history plays as well.

Critics have disagreed on the form, structure, and ultimate meaning of the play. The title character is killed halfway through the action, and a distinguished hero is questionable. The climax is a bit out of place, and Shakespeare gives no clear indication as to whose side he favors in the conflict. Some critics even question the play's fundamental purpose. One thing at least is clear, however: Shakespeare made a conscious decision in this play not to present a shining hero who leads a life of brilliance and glory, as it seems he did in *Henry V*, which appeared in the same year. *Julius Caesar* is a political play, and Shakespeare develops his characters carefully on all sides of the sociopolitical debate. Therefore not only viewers and readers but also directors and producers must make up their own minds as they interpret the play.

Julius Caesar has been popular with audiences everywhere, in theaters and in classrooms—beginning in Shakespeare's day, when Roman history and literature were already absorbed into English culture. And in recent times, it has been the most often quoted play by critics devoted to political theory or philosophy. It describes a basic, prototypical situation, one that can be—and has been—used to extrapolate the developing facets of modern life.

The driving conflict in the play is tyranny versus a republic. For the Elizabethans, it should be noted, *tyranny* always meant despotic abuse of power; *republic* meant a representative form of government, or a state in which at least some of the people would have a vote. (The US government was patterned after the Roman Republic.) Neither the Middle Ages nor the Renaissance cared much for democratic governments. Thus Dante Alighieri (1265–1321), famous for his vision of the afterlife in his epic poem "The Divine Comedy," placed Brutus in the ice-covered pit of Hell, dangling from Satan's mouth, as one of the world's greatest betrayers, along with Cassius and Judas Iscariot. By contrast Shakespeare shifted the emphasis, giving essentially equal weight to both sides.

England also faced great dangers in 1599: the aging queen, sixty-five years old and obviously nearing the end of her life, still had not named a successor—possibly paving the way for more bloody wars of inheritance and terrible religious conflicts. England at this time looked back on a century of such problems.

In addition Elizabeth's current favorite, Robert Devereux, the Earl of Essex, a handsome and chivalrous young man with ambitious dreams, offered additional fears. He had just returned from Ireland, where he had been sent to put down the latest rebellion, but he bungled the job and neglected his duty. And worst of all, instead of wiping out the enemy, he made a truce with the Irish leader, the Earl of Tyrone, which was interpreted at home as humiliating to England, a mistake for which he suffered considerably. In 1601 Essex attempted to usurp the throne, was arrested, tried, and executed for treason. Even Globe personnel were arrested and questioned because they staged the meaningful *Richard II* just before the rebellion, allegedly to rally support. Furthermore, some Englishmen at the end of the sixteenth century had good reason to see the problems of Shakespeare's Rome as a mirror image of their own and to be nervous as a result.

In the first chapter of this volume, three current biographers relate events in Shakespeare's life, especially as they reflect on the creation of *Julius Caesar*. Chapter Two explores the complicated political setting and relationships in the play, and diverse authors discuss the controversial issue of tyranny. Finally Chapter Three investigates analogous situations that exist in countries throughout the world today.

Chronology

500 B.C.

The Roman Republic is established. Constant warfare and class struggles follow.

133 B.C.

Tiberius Gracchus, tribune, attempts to redistribute land and allow the poor to own land. He is murdered by wealthy and hostile patricians along with about three hundred of his followers.

123–122 B.C.

Gaius Gracchus (younger brother of Tiberius Gracchus), after being elected as tribune in two consecutive years, continues his brother's populist land reforms and attempts to change the system of justice.

121 B.C.

Gaius leads a demonstration after losing an election to become tribune for what would have been his third consecutive year and is stormed and killed, along with about three thousand of his followers, by the same aristocratic enemies.

107–49 B.C.

Rome, ruled by powerful generals, is in constant turmoil and warfare.

49 B.C.

Julius Caesar defeats and destroys Pompey.

49–44 B.C.

Caesar rules as dictator.

44 B.C.
Caesar is made dictator for life but is assassinated.

1558
Elizabeth I ascends the throne.

1564
William Shakespeare is born in Stratford-upon-Avon.

1567
In Scotland, Mary Queen of Scots is deposed and eleven-month-old James ascends the throne.

1576
The Theatre (the first professional theater in England) opens north of London.

1582
Shakespeare marries Anne Hathaway.

1585–1592
This time period is considered by Shakespeare scholars to be his lost years. Little about his life during these years is known with any certainty.

Shakespeare goes to London without his family and sees heads of dissidents on London Bridge as he enters the city.

His first plays are performed.

1587
Mary, Queen of Scots, is executed for conspiring against Elizabeth.

1590–1592
Three parts of *Henry VI* are presented.

1593
London is hit by the plague, which leads to theaters being closed.

1593–94

Shakespeare writes *The Rape of Lucrece*, and *Titus Andronicus* and *The Taming of the Shrew* are produced.

1594

The Comedy of Errors is performed.

Shakespeare acquires a share in the Lord Chamberlain's men (a theater company), beginning a successful career as an investor in theaters.

1599

The Earl of Essex, given chief command in Ireland to suppress a revolt, is accused of blundering and abusing power and comes home in disgrace.

Shakespeare acquires one-tenth of the Globe Theatre.

The first production at the Globe is *Julius Caesar*. *Henry V* is produced.

1598–1600

As You Like It, *Much Ado About Nothing*, *The Merry Wives of Windsor*, and *Henry IV, Part 2* are produced.

1601

The Earl of Essex is executed in the Tower of London after a failed attempt to take over the throne. Globe personnel are arrested, questioned, and released.

Shakespeare's father dies after much trouble and investigation as a possible secret Catholic.

1602

Twelfth Night is produced.

1603

Elizabeth dies and James VI of Scotland ascends the English throne as James I. He is a scholar, an expert on witchcraft, and a believer in the divine right of kings.

Shakespeare's company becomes the King's Men.

1604
Measure for Measure and *Othello* are produced.

1605
The Gunpowder Plot, in which Catholic rebels planned to blow up parliament, is discovered, resulting in panic and the persecution of Catholics.

1605–1606
King Lear is produced; *Macbeth* is presented before King James.

1606–1608
Pericles is performed at court. *Antony and Cleopatra, Coriolanus, The Winter's Tale,* and *Cymbeline* are produced.

1609
Shakespeare's company purchases Blackfriars Theatre.

1610–1611
The Tempest is produced, and Shakespeare moves to Stratford.

1613
Henry VIII is produced.

The Globe is destroyed by fire during a performance of *Henry VIII*. It reopens the following year.

1616
Shakespeare dies on April 23.

1623
The First Folio edition of Shakespeare's works is published.

CHAPTER 1

Background on
William Shakespeare

The Life of Shakespeare

John F. Andrews

John F. Andrews is the author of many books and articles on Shakespeare. He founded and served as chief executive officer of the Shakespeare Guild and was editor of the Shakespeare Quarterly.

A fellow playwright called William Shakespeare a man "for all time," and Shakespeare's cultural influence has persisted for roughly four hundred years after his death. In this selection Andrews chronicles Shakespeare's life and career up until the creation of Julius Caesar. *As a young boy of a prominent family, Shakespeare would have been eligible for a classical education into his teenage years. Only after his marriage to Anne Hathaway and the birth of their three children did Shakespeare travel to London and begin his acting and writing career. Andrews presents the excitement and the controversies of late-sixteenth- and early-seventeenth-century London as the setting for Shakespeare's dramatic works. He then introduces some of the classical and Renaissance writings that likely influenced Shakespeare in his conception of* Julius Caesar. *Even into the twentieth century, fresh perspectives on Shakespeare's views and intentions surfaced.*

"He was not of an age, but for all time." So wrote [fellow playwright] Ben Jonson in his dedicatory verses to the memory of William Shakespeare in 1623, and so we continue to affirm today. No other writer, in English or in any other language, can rival the appeal that Shakespeare has enjoyed. And no one else in any artistic endeavor has projected a cultural influence as broad or as deep. . . .

Biographers Can Know Few Details for Sure

One thing we do know is that if Shakespeare was a man for all time, he was also very much a man of his own age. Christened at Holy Trinity Church in Stratford-upon-Avon on 26 April 1564, he grew up as the eldest of five children reared by John Shakespeare, a tradesman who played an increasingly active role in the town's civic affairs as his business prospered, and Mary Arden Shakespeare, the daughter of a gentleman farmer from nearby Wilmcote. Whether Shakespeare was born on 23 April, as tradition holds, is not known; but a birth date only a few days prior to the recorded baptism seems eminently probable, particularly in view of the fear his parents must have had that William, like two sisters who had preceded him and one who followed, might die in infancy. By the time young William was old enough to begin attending school, he had a younger brother (Gilbert, born in 1566) and a baby sister (Joan, born in 1569). As he attained his youth, he found himself with two more brothers to help look after (Richard, born in 1574, and Edmund, born in 1580), the younger of whom eventually followed his by-then-prominent eldest brother to London and the theater, where he had a brief career as an actor before his untimely death at twenty-seven.

The house where Shakespeare spent his childhood stood adjacent to the wool shop in which his father plied a successful trade as a glover and dealer in leather goods and other commodities. Before moving to Stratford sometime prior to 1552 (when the records show that he was fined for failing to remove a dunghill from outside his house to the location where refuse was normally to be deposited), John Shakespeare had been a farmer in the neighboring village of Snitterfield. Whether he was able to read and write is uncertain. He executed official documents, not with his name, but with a cross signifying his glover's compasses. Some scholars interpret this as a "signature" that might have been considered more "authentic" than a full autograph; others have taken it to be an indication of illiteracy. But even if John Shakespeare was not one of the "learned," he was certainly a man of what a later age would call upward mobility. By marrying Mary Arden, the daughter of his father's landlord, he acquired the benefits of a better social standing and a lucrative inheritance, much of which he invested in property (he bought several houses). And by involving himself in public service, he rose by sure degrees to the highest municipal positions Stratford had to offer: chamberlain (1561), alderman (1565), and bailiff (or mayor) and justice of the peace (1568). A few years after his elevation to the office of bailiff, probably around 1576, John Shakespeare approached the College of Heralds for armorial bearings and the right to call himself a gentleman. Before his application was acted upon, however, his fortunes took a sudden turn for the worse, and it was not until 1596, when his eldest son had attained some status and renewed the petition, that a Shakespeare coat of arms was finally granted. This must have been a comfort to John Shakespeare in his declining years (he died in 1601). . . .

The records we do have suggest that during young William's formative years he enjoyed the advantages that would have accrued to him as the son of one of the most influential citizens of a bustling market town in the fertile Midlands. When he was taken to services at Holy Trinity Church, he would have sat with his family in the front pew, in accordance with his father's civic rank. There he would have heard and felt the words and rhythms of the Bible, the sonorous phrases of the 1559 Book of Common Prayer, the exhortations of the Homilies. In all likelihood, after spending a year or two at a "petty school" to learn the rudiments of reading and writing, he would have proceeded, at the age of seven, to "grammar school." Given his father's social position, young William would have been eligible to attend the King's New School, located above the Guild Hall and adjacent to the Guild Chapel (institutions that would both have been quite familiar to a man with the elder Shakespeare's municipal duties), no more than a five-minute walk from the Shakespeare house on Henley Street. Though no records survive to tell us who attended the Stratford grammar school during this period, we do know that it had well-qualified and comparatively well-paid masters; and, through the painstaking research of such scholars as T.W. Baldwin, we now recognize that a curriculum such as the one offered at the King's New School would have equipped its pupils with what by modern standards would be a rather formidable classical education.

During his many long school days there, young Shakespeare would have become thoroughly grounded in Latin, acquired some background in Greek, and developed enough linguistic facility to pick up whatever he may have wanted later from such modern languages as Italian and French. Along the way he would have become familiar with such authors as Aesop, Caesar, Cicero, Sallust, Livy, Virgil, Horace, Ovid, and Seneca. He would have studied logic and rhetoric as well as grammar, and he would have been taught the principles of composition and oratory from the writings of such masters as Quintilian and Erasmus. . . .

A Choice of the Stage over Marriage and Fatherhood

Once his school years ended, Shakespeare married, at eighteen, a woman who was eight years his senior. We know that Anne Hathaway was pregnant when the marriage license was issued by the Bishop of Worcester on 27 November 1582, because a daughter, Susanna, was baptized in Holy Trinity six months later on 26 May 1583. We have good reason to believe that the marriage was hastily arranged. . . .

What we do have to go on is certainly compatible with the suspicion that William and Anne were somewhat less than ardent lovers. They had only two more children—the twins,

Playwright William Shakespeare examined tyranny in some of his works.

Hamnet and Judith, baptized on 2 February 1585—and they lived more than a hundred miles apart, so far as we can tell, for the better part of the twenty-year period during which Shakespeare was employed in the London theater. . . .

Naturally we would like to know more about what Shakespeare was like as a husband and family man. But most of us would give just as much to know what took place in his life between 1585 (when the parish register shows him to have become the father of twins) and 1592 (when we find the earliest surviving reference to him as a rising star in the London theater). What did he do during these so-called "dark years"? Did he study law, as some have suspected? Did he travel on the Continent? Did he become an apprentice to a butcher, as one late-seventeenth-century account had it? Or—most plausibly, in the view of many modern biographers—did he teach school for a while? All we can say for certain is that by the time his children were making their own way to school in rural Stratford, William Shakespeare had become an actor and writer in what was already the largest city in Europe.

Shakespeare probably traveled the hundred miles to London by way of the spires of Oxford, as do most visitors returning from Stratford to London today. But why he went, or when, history does not tell us. It has been plausibly suggested that he joined an acting troupe (the Queen's Men) that was one player short when it toured Stratford in 1587. If so, he may have migrated by way of one or two intermediary companies to a position with the troupe that became the Lord Chamberlain's Men in 1594. The only thing we can assert with any assurance is that by 1592 Shakespeare had established himself as an actor and had written at least three plays. . . .

The Context for Shakespeare's Plays

In Shakespeare's day London was a vigorous city of somewhere between 150,000 and 200,000 inhabitants. If in its more majestic aspects it was dominated by the court of Queen Elizabeth, in its everyday affairs it was accented by the hustle and bustle of getting and spending. Its Royal Exchange was one of the forerunners of today's stock exchanges. Its many market-places offered a variety of goods for a variety of tastes.

Its crowded streets presented a colorful pageant of Elizabethan modes of transport and dress, ranging from countrywomen in homespun to elegant ladies in apparel as decorative as their husbands' wealth—and the Queen's edicts on clothing—would allow. Its inns and taverns afforded a rich diversity of vivid personalities—eating, tippling, chatting, and enjoying games and pleasures of all kinds. It was, in short, an immensely stimulating social and cultural environment, and we can be sure that Shakespeare took full advantage of the opportunity it gave him to observe humanity in all its facets. Like Prince Hal, he must have learned "to drink with any tinker in his own language," and it was this as much as anything he was taught at school (or might have acquired by attendance at university) that equipped him to create such vibrant characters as Mistress Quickly, proud Hotspur, and the imperturbable Bottom.

Not that all was always well. Like any major city, London also had its problems. . . . London's Puritan authorities, regarding the theaters as dens of iniquity, closed them down on any available pretext, particularly when the plague was rampant. Meanwhile, even without the plague or the theaters to concern them (and one gathers that some of the authorities were anything but sure about which was the greater peril), the city fathers had to contend with gambling drunkenness, prostitution, and other vices, especially in the Bankside district south of the Thames and in the other "liberties" outside the city walls to the west, east, and north (such as Shoreditch, where James Burbage had erected the first permanent commercial play-house, the Theatre, when Shakespeare was only twelve, and where many of Shakespeare's plays prior to 1599 were first performed). Here most blatantly, but elsewhere as well, pickpockets, vagabonds, and other members of the fraternity of urban lowlife lay in wait for "conies," as they called their unsuspecting victims. . . .

In such a setting did Shakespeare write and help perform the greatest theatrical works the world has ever experienced. And he did so in suburbs known primarily for entertainments that we would regard as totally alien from the sweet Swan of Avon's poetic grace. For if Shoreditch and, later, Bankside were to blossom into the finest theatrical centers of that or any other age, they were also, for better or worse, the seedbeds for such brutal spectator sports as bearbaiting, bullbaiting, and cockfighting. This may help account for the blood and violence so frequently displayed on the Elizabethan stage, most notably in such early Shakespearean experiments as the *Henry VI* trilogy and *Titus Andronicus*, but also in mature works such as *Julius Caesar* and *King Lear*. But of course there was a good deal more than murder and mayhem in the "wooden O" that served as amphitheatre for most of Shakespeare's dramatic productions. . . .

Shakespeare's Early Tragic Plays

Shakespeare's middle years are notable for sophisticated achievements in the genre we now refer to as romantic comedy, [and] they are equally notable for the playwright's unprecedented strides in the development of two other genres: tragedy and tragicomedy. In 1599, probably at the Globe, the Lord Chamberlain's Men offered the earliest recorded performance of *Julius Caesar* (the first of three mature tragedies, now grouped as "the Roman Plays," which all saw print for the first time in the 1623 Folio). Two years later, in late 1600 or early 1601, the company probably added to its repertory *Hamlet*. Then in late 1601 or early 1602—once again drawing on the "classical" matter that had been the basis for the action of *Julius Caesar* and for many of the allusions in *Hamlet*—Shakespeare completed *Troilus and Cressida*, a play so uncompromisingly "intellectual" in its insistence that the audience "by indirections find directions out" that critics from the seventeenth century to the present have found it all but impossible to classify. . . .

Julius Caesar—a play that may owe something to sources as seemingly remote as [ancient Roman philosopher] St. Augustine's *City of God* and [Renaissance humanist and priest] Erasmus's *Praise of Folly* in addition to such obvious classical antecedents as [ancient Greek and Roman historian] Plutarch's *Lives* and [ancient Roman senator and historian] Tacitus's *Annals*—is now regarded as a dramatic work of considerable complexity. On the one hand, the play captures with remarkable fidelity the ethos and rhetorical style of late-republican Rome—so much so, indeed, that it may be said that Shakespeare's portraits of Caesar and his contemporaries have largely formed our own impressions of how the ancient Romans thought and talked and conducted their civic affairs. Recent studies of the play's references to "philosophy" indicate, moreover, that Shakespeare knew a good deal about Roman Stoicism and perceived it as one of the characterizing traits that differentiated Brutus from Cassius, an Epicurean continually nonplussed by his companion's mental rigidity and emotional aloofness.

But if Shakespeare brought to his dramatic art a historical imagination capable of reconstructing a self-consistent Roman world—and one that was distinct in significant ways from his own Elizabethan England—he was also capable of embodying in his representation of that world a perspective that amounted, in effect, to a Renaissance humanist critique of pre-Christian civilization. Thus it was quite possible for Shakespeare to portray the conspirators and their cause, as it were, "sympathetically"—so much so, indeed, that a twentieth-century audience, unwittingly misreading the play, finds it almost impossible not to hear in such exclamations as "peace, freedom, and liberty!" the precursors of America's own founding fathers. At the same time, however, Shakespeare would have known that he could rely on his Elizabethan contemporaries to regard as foredoomed any attempt to achieve social harmony through what they would have seen on the stage as bloody butchery and regicide. By the same token, of course, Shakespeare could encourage his audience to "identify" with Brutus through participation in his soliloquies, while simultaneously assuming that alert members of that audience would recognize that Brutus's thought processes are often misguided and self-deceptive.

In the late 1930s [American writer and critic] Mark Van Doren observed that, whatever Brutus's positive qualities as a high-minded patriot, he tends to come across in the play as a self-righteous, almost pharisaical prig, particularly in the quarrel scene with Cassius. In recent years a number of scholars have confirmed the validity of Van Doren's perception by showing that it is consistent with the hypothesis that in his portrayal of Brutus Shakespeare was drawing on a widely held Christian tradition that regarded Stoicism as a philosophy that rendered its adherents hard-hearted, arrogant, and so assured of their own virtue as to be largely incapable of recognizing or repenting of their faults. If this reading of Brutus is closer to Shakespeare's intention than the more sentimental view that approaches everything in the play from the retrospective vantage-point of Mark Antony's eulogy for "the noblest Roman of them all," it tends to cast much of *Julius Caesar* in an ironic light—and by implication to require an audience alert to clues that are not always so self-evident as a twentieth-century reader or viewer might expect.

Shakespeare Travels to London, a City of Power and Politics

Stephen Greenblatt

A playwright and Cogan University Professor of the Humanities at Harvard University, Stephen Greenblatt is regarded as one of the founders of the New Historicism, a branch of literary theory. He is the author of numerous books on William Shakespeare.

In this excerpt from his biography Will in the World, *Greenblatt addresses Shakespeare's youthful antiauthoritarianism and his later confrontation with London's harsh political conditions. Before Shakespeare's journey to London, he enjoyed poaching on the estate of the powerful Sir Thomas Lucy, later making Lucy the subject of a satiric poem. Greenblatt speculates that when Shakespeare first arrived in London, he would have witnessed the heads of insurgents stuck on pikes around bridges. Many of these were Catholics, like those in Shakespeare's family, who failed to pay allegiance to the Church of England. The policy that resulted in this cruel intolerance was introduced by none other than Thomas Lucy, the man on whose land he poached. This sight, writes Greenblatt, may have had a role in moderating Shakespeare's rebelliousness. The sight of the raucous city may also have inspired his mob scenes in* Julius Caesar.

In the summer of 1583 the nineteen-year-old William Shakespeare was settling into the life of a married man with a newborn daughter, living all together with his parents and his sister, Joan, and his brothers, Gilbert, Richard, and Edmund, and however many servants they could afford in the spacious house on Henley Street. He may have been working in the glover's shop, perhaps, or making a bit of money as a teacher's or lawyer's assistant. In his spare time he must have continued to write poetry, practice the lute, hone his skills as a fencer—that is, work on his ability to impersonate the lifestyle of a gentleman. His northern sojourn, assuming he had one, was behind him. If in Lancashire he had begun a career as a professional player, he must, for the moment at least, have put it aside. And if he had had a brush with the dark world of Catholic conspiracy, sainthood, and martyrdom . . . he must still more decisively have turned away from it with a shudder. He had embraced ordinariness, or ordinariness had embraced him.

Shakespeare's Mysterious Departure from Stratford

Then sometime in the mid-1580s (the precise date is not known), he tore himself away from his family, left Stratford-upon-Avon, and made his way to London. How or why he took this momentous step is unclear, though until recently biographers were generally content with a story first recorded in the late seventeenth century by the clergyman Richard Davies. Davies wrote that Shakespeare was "much given to all unluckiness in stealing venison and rabbits, particularly from Sir—— Lucy, who had him oft whipped and sometimes imprisoned and at last made him fly his native country to his great advancement." The early-eighteenth-century biographer and editor Nicholas Rowe printed a similar account of the "Extravagance" that forced Shakespeare "both out of his country and that way of living which he had taken up." Will had, in Rowe's account, fallen into bad company: he began to consort with youths who made a practice of deer poaching; in their company, he went more than once to rob Sir Thomas Lucy's park at Charlecote, about four miles from Stratford.

For this he was prosecuted by that gentleman, as he thought, somewhat too severely; and in order to revenge that ill usage, he made a ballad upon him. And though this, probably the first essay of his poetry, be lost, yet it is said to have been so very bitter, that it redoubled the prosecution against him to that degree, that he was obliged to leave his business and family in Warwickshire, for some time, and shelter himself in London. . . .

While Lucy did not keep an enclosed park at the time that Shakespeare would have been caught poaching, he did maintain a warren, an enclosed area where rabbits and other game, possibly including deer, could breed. And he was evidently not indifferent to his property rights: he hired keepers to protect the game and watch for poachers, and he introduced a bill in Parliament in 1584 against poaching. As for whipping, it may not have been a legal punishment, but the justice of the peace may have been inclined to teach the young offender a lesson, particularly if he suspected that the poacher and his parents might be recusants. No doubt it would have been improper for Sir Thomas Lucy, as justice of the peace, to sit in judgment on a case in which he himself was the alleged victim, but it would be naive to imagine that local magnates always stayed within the letter of the law or carefully avoided conflicts of interest. After all, the story refers to Shakespeare's sense of ill-usage—that is, to his being treated worse than he felt he deserved to be treated for what he was caught doing.

The question, then, is not the degree of evidence but rather the imaginative life that the incident has, the access it gives to something important in Shakespeare's life and work. The particular act with which he was charged has by now ceased to have much meaning, and the story correspondingly has begun to drop away from biographies. But in Shakespeare's time and into the eighteenth century the idea of deer poaching had a special resonance; it was good to think with, a powerful tool for reconstructing the sequence of events that led the young man to leave Stratford.

The Thrill of a Risk

For Elizabethans deer poaching was not understood princi-
pally as having to do with hunger; it was a story not about
desperation but about risk. Oxford students were famous for
this escapade. It was, for a start, a daring game: it took impressive skill and cool nerves to trespass on a powerful person's
land, kill a large animal, and drag it away, without getting
caught by those who patrolled the area. "What, hast not thou
full often struck a doe," someone asks in one of Shakespeare's
early plays, "And borne her cleanly by the keeper's nose?"
(*Titus Andronicus*). It was a skillful assault upon property, a
symbolic violation of the social order, a coded challenge to
authority. That challenge was supposed to be kept within
bounds: the game involved cunning and an awareness of limits. After all, one was not supposed to beat up the keeper—
then misdemeanor turns into felony—and one was not supposed to get caught. Deer poaching was about the pleasures of
hunting and killing but also about the pleasures of stealth and
trickery, about knowing how far to go, about contriving to get
away with something.

Throughout Shakespeare's career as a playwright he was a
brilliant poacher—deftly entering into territory marked out by
others, taking for himself what he wanted, and walking away
with his prize under the keeper's nose. He was particularly
good at seizing and making his own the property of the elite,
the music, the gestures, the language. This is only a metaphor,
of course; it is not evidence that young Will engaged in actual
poaching. What we know, and what those who originally circulated the legend knew, is that he had a complex attitude toward authority, at once sly, genially submissive, and subtly
challenging. He was capable of devastating criticism; he saw
through lies, hypocrisies, and distortions; he undermined virtually all of the claims that those in power made for themselves. And yet he was easygoing, humorous, pleasantly indirect, almost apologetic. If this relation to authority was not

simply implanted in him, if it was more likely something he learned, then his formative learning experience may well have been a nasty encounter with one of the principal authorities in his district.

The Prime Weapon of the Powerless

For in all the versions of the story something went wrong: Shakespeare was caught and then treated more harshly than he felt was appropriate (and indeed than the law allowed). He responded, it is said, with a bitter ballad. Versions of the ballad have predictably surfaced—none of them interesting as poetry or believable as Shakespeare's actual verses. "If lowsie is Lucy, as some volke miscalle it, / Then Lucy is lowsie whatever befall it," etc. More interesting is the idea that Shakespeare must have responded to harsh treatment with an insulting piece of writing, presumably an attack on Lucy's character or the honor of his wife.

Modern biographers are skeptical largely because they believe that Shakespeare was not that kind of person and that Lucy was both too powerful and too respectable to be slandered. "In public feared and respected, Sir Thomas in his domestic affairs appears to have been not unamiable," observes one of Shakespeare's most amiable and brilliant biographers, Samuel Schoenbaum. "He wrote testimonial letters for an honest gentlewoman and an ailing servant." But the late-seventeenth-century gossips who circulated the story may have had a better understanding of that world. They grasped that a man like Lucy could combine geniality and public-spiritedness—entertaining the queen at Charlecote, keeping a company of players, acting boldly and decisively in times of plague—with ruthless violence. They knew that it was dangerous to write anything against a person in authority—you could be charged with "scandalium magnatum," slandering an official—and at the same time that such writing was the prime weapon of the powerless. Above all, they believed that something serious must have driven Shakespeare out of Stratford, something more than his own poetic dreams and theatrical skill, something more than dissatisfaction with his marriage, and something more than the limited economic opportunities in the immediate area.

They doubted, in other words, that Shakespeare simply wandered off to London in search of new opportunities. Whether he was helping in his father's failing business, or working as a poor scrivener (a noverint, as it was sometimes called) in a lawyer's office, or teaching the rudiments of Latin grammar to schoolboys, they believed that without some shock Shakespeare would have continued in the rut that life had prepared for him. With the family's lands mortgaged, his education finished, no profession, a wife and three children to support, he had already begun to deepen that rut for himself. Rumormongers heard something that led them to believe that trouble with authority drove him out and that the authority in question was Sir Thomas Lucy. They thought too that something Shakespeare wrote was involved in the trouble. . . .

Shakespeare was a master of double consciousness. He was a man who spent his money on a coat of arms but who mocked the pretentiousness of such a claim; a man who invested in real estate but who ridiculed in *Hamlet* precisely such an entrepreneur as he himself was; a man who spent his life and his deepest energies on the theater but who laughed at the theater and regretted making himself a show. Though Shakespeare seems to have recycled every word he ever encountered, every person he ever met, every experience he ever had—it is difficult otherwise to explain the enormous richness of his work—he contrived at the same time to hide himself from view, to ward off vulnerability, to forswear intimacy. And in the case of his encounter with Thomas Lucy, he may, by the late 1590s, have buried inside light public laughter the traces of an intense fear that had once gripped him. . . .

Escaping to London

There were other bustling cities in England, and, if he had traveled, the young Shakespeare could conceivably have seen one or two of them, but none was like London. With a population nearing two hundred thousand, it was some fifteen times larger than the next most populous cities in England and Wales; in all of Europe only Naples and Paris exceeded it in size. Its commercial vitality was intense: London, as one contemporary put it, was "the Fair that lasts all year." This meant that it was fast escaping the seasonal rhythms by which the rest of the country lived; and it was escaping too the deep sense of the local that governed identity elsewhere. It was one of the only places in England where you were not surrounded by people who knew you, your family, and many of the most intimate details of your life, one of the only places in which your clothes and food and furniture were not produced by people you knew personally. It was in consequence the preeminent site not only of relative anonymity but also of fantasy: a place where you could dream of escaping your origins and turning into someone else.

That Shakespeare had this dream is virtually certain: it lies at the heart of what it means to be an actor, it is essential to the craft of the playwright, and it fuels the willingness of audiences to part with their pennies in order to see a play. He may also have had more private motives, a desire to escape whatever had led him into difficulties with Thomas Lucy, a desire to escape his wife and his three children, a desire to escape the glove and illegal wool trade of his improvident father. In his plays, he repeatedly staged scenes of characters separated from their familial bonds, stripped of their identities, stumbling into unfamiliar territory. . . .

Rebels, Reform, and Mob Rule

In his very early history play *2 Henry VI*, Shakespeare depicted a band of lower-class Kentish rebels, led by the clothworker

Jack Cade, descending on London to overthrow the social order. Cade promises a kind of primitive economic reform: "There shall be in England seven halfpenny loaves sold for a penny, the three-hooped pot shall have ten hoops, and I will make it felony to drink small beer." The rebels—"a ragged multitude / Of hinds and peasants, rude and merciless"— want to burn the records of the realm, abolish literacy, break into prisons and free the prisoners, make the fountains run with wine, execute the gentry. "The first thing we do," famously says one of Cade's followers, "let's kill all the lawyers."

In a sequence of wild scenes, poised between grotesque comedy and nightmare, the young Shakespeare imagined— and invited his audience to imagine—what it would be like to have London controlled by a half-mad, belligerently illiterate rabble from the country. Something about the fantasy seems to have released a current of personal energy in the neophyte playwright, himself only recently arrived in the capital. While the upper-class characters in this early history play are for the most part stiff and unconvincing—the king in particular is almost completely a cipher—the lower-class rebels are startlingly vital. It is as if Shakespeare had grasped something crucial for the writing of plays: he could split apart elements of himself and his background, mold each of them into vivid form, and then at once laugh, shudder, and destroy them. . . .

And it is the London crowd—the unprecedented concentration of bodies jostling through the narrow streets, crossing and recrossing the great bridge, pressing into taverns and churches and theaters—that is the key to the whole spectacle. The sight of all those people—along with their noise, the smell of their breath, their rowdiness and potential for violence—seems to have been Shakespeare's first and most enduring impression of the great city. In *Julius Caesar*, he returned to the spectacle of the bloodthirsty mob, roaming the streets in search of the conspirators who have killed their hero Caesar:

THIRD PLEBEIAN: Your name, sir, truly.

CINNA: Truly, my name is Cinna.

FIRST PLEBEIAN: Tear him to pieces! He's a conspirator.

CINNA: I am Cinna the poet, I am Cinna the poet.

FOURTH PLEBEIAN: Tear him for his bad verses, tear him for his bad verses.

CINNA: I am not Cinna the conspirator.

FOURTH PLEBEIAN: It is no matter, his name's Cinna. Pluck but his name out of his heart, and turn him going.

THIRD PLEBEIAN: Tear him, tear him!

This urban mob, rioting for bread and threatening to overturn the social order, figures as well in *Coriolanus* [one of Shakespeare's "Roman plays"]. And it is this same mob—"Mechanic slaves / With greasy aprons, rules, and hammers"—that Cleopatra imagines watching her being led captive through the streets of the great city [in *Antony and Cleopatra*]. The very thought of smelling their "thick breaths," as they cheer the triumph of Rome, is enough to confirm her in her determination to commit suicide.

Even when his scene is Rome, Ephesus, Vienna, or Venice, Shakespeare's fixed point of urban reference was London. Ancient Romans may have worn togas and gone hatless, but when the rioting plebeians in *Coriolanus* get what they want, they throw their caps in the air, just as Elizabethan Londoners did. . . .

The Sight That Met the Young Rebel

Saint Magnus' Corner was at the northern end of London Bridge, the place where Shakespeare himself may have first set foot in the city. He would, in all likelihood, have been traveling with the troupe of actors he had joined. Perhaps, as they approached the capital, they joked about the rebellious butchers and weavers who long ago had marched on London. The playing company, in any case, would have wanted to attract attention to themselves, to let the populace know that they were back in the city and that they were performing at a particular place and time. In their gaudiest clothes, beating drums and waving flags, they would have timed their arrival and sought the busiest route; if they were approaching from the south, they would have marched up Southwark High Street and across London Bridge.

This, then, might well have been Shakespeare's initial glimpse of London: an architectural marvel, some eight hundred feet in length, that a French visitor, Etienne Perlin, called "the most beautiful bridge in the world." The congested roadway, supported on twenty piers of stone sixty feet high and thirty broad, was lined with tall houses and shops extending out over the water on struts. Many of the shops sold luxury goods—fine silks, hosiery, velvet caps—and some of the buildings themselves commanded attention: you could buy groceries in a two-story thirteenth-century stone building that had formerly been a chantry dedicated to St. Thomas à Becket where Masses were once sung for the souls of the dead. From the breaks between the buildings there were splendid views up and down the great river, especially to the west; overhead there were scavenging birds, wheeling in the air; and in the river hundreds of swans, plucked once a year for the queen's bedding and upholstery.

But one sight in particular would certainly have arrested Shakespeare's attention; it was a major tourist attraction, always pointed out to new arrivals. Stuck on poles on the Great Stone Gate, two arches from the Southwark side, were severed heads, some completely reduced to skulls, others parboiled and tanned, still identifiable. These were not the remains of common thieves, rapists, and murderers. Ordinary criminals were strung up by the hundreds on gibbets located around the margins of the city. The heads on the bridge, visitors were duly informed, were those of gentlemen and nobles who suffered the fate of traitors. A foreign visitor to London in 1592 counted thirty-four of them; another in 1598 said he counted more than thirty. When he first walked across the bridge, or very soon after, Shakespeare must have realized that among the heads were those of [conspirators] John Somerville and the man who bore his own mother's name and may have been his distant kinsman, Edward Arden.

Confronting Political Terror

A father and his son-in-law, their severed heads grinning on poles across from one another. "Let them kiss one another, for they loved well when they were alive." The severed heads he saw on the bridge must have made an impact upon his imagination, and not only as demonstrated in the Cade scenes of *2 Henry VI*. If he had spent some dangerous months in Lancashire, Shakespeare would already have imbibed powerful lessons about danger and the need for discretion, concealment, and fiction. These lessons would have been reinforced in Stratford, as tensions rose and rumors of conspiracy, assassination, and invasion spread. But the sight on the bridge was the most compelling instruction yet: keep control of yourself; do not fall into the hands of your enemies; be smart, tough, and realistic; master strategies of concealment and evasion; keep your head on your shoulders.

Hard lessons for a poet and an actor aspiring to be heard and seen by the world. But some such lessons may have caused Shakespeare to reach a decision that has since made it difficult to understand who he was. Where are his personal letters? Why have scholars, ferreting for centuries, failed to find the books he must have owned—or rather, why did he choose not to write his name in those books, the way that [English writers Ben] Jonson or [John] Donne or many of his [other] contemporaries did? Why, in the huge, glorious body of his writing, is there no direct access to his thoughts about politics or religion or art? Why is everything he wrote—even in the sonnets—couched in a way that enables him to hide his face and his innermost thoughts? Scholars have long thought that the answer must lie in indifference and accident: no contemporary thought that this playwright's personal views were sufficiently important to record, no one bothered to save his casual letters, and the boxes of papers that may have been left to his daughter Susanna were eventually sold off and used to wrap fish or stiffen the spines of new books or were simply burned. Possibly. But the heads on the pikes may have spoken to him on the day he entered London—and he may well have heeded their warning.

Shakespeare's Fascination with Rulers

Peter Ackroyd

Peter Ackroyd, an English biographer and novelist, is the chief book reviewer for the Times *of London. His books include* Thames, *a history of the river that flows through central London.*

The Globe Theatre, in which William Shakespeare had both an artistic and a professional interest, presented Julius Caesar *on June 12, 1599. According to Ackroyd in the following excerpt, astrological considerations—as important to Elizabethans as they were to Caesar and the Romans—played a part in setting the premiere. In* Julius Caesar, *his first of three "Roman" plays, Shakespeare creates an ambiguous dictator and puzzling reformers—characteristics unfamiliar to plays written by his contemporaries. Writers of the period referred to Shakespeare's version of the tragedy and even satirized it, but Caesar is only one example of Shakespeare's careful treatment of kings and other rulers. Ackroyd argues that in Shakespeare's plays, whether tragic or comedic, he tends to sympathize with his kingly characters. Ackroyd even wonders if Shakespeare daydreamed of power and was attracted to the stage because of the similarities he saw between kings and players. Furthermore, Shakespeare received many court favors and was officially recognized as "the king's true servant."*

A horoscope was consulted to determine the exact day for the opening of the Globe. The play chosen for that auspicious occasion was *Julius Caesar* and, from allusions in the text itself, it is clear that it was first performed on the after-

noon of 12 June 1599. This was the day of the summer sol-
stice and the appearance of a new moon. A new moon was
deemed by astrologers to be the most opportune time "to
open a new house." There was a high tide at Southwark early
that afternoon, which helped to expedite the journey of the
playgoers coming from the north of the river. That evening,
after sunset, Venus and Jupiter appeared in the sky. These may
seem to be matters of arcane calculation but to the actors and
playgoers of the late sixteenth century they were very significant indeed. It has been demonstrated, for example, that the
axis of the Globe is 48 degrees east of true north, and so was
in fact in direct alignment with the midsummer sunrise. Astrological lore was a familiar and formative influence upon all
the affairs of daily life. It is also the context for the supernatu-
ral visitations and prognostications in *Julius Caesar* itself.

There is other evidence of the play's summer opening. In
June 1599 the takings at Philip Henslowe's Rose, neighbour to
the new Globe, registered a sharp fall which must have been
the result of new competition. It is a matter of record that
Henslowe and the actor-manager Alleyn soon decided to de-
part with the Admiral's Men from the Rose, and to resume
acting at the newly built Fortune in the northern suburbs.
The proximity to the Lord Chamberlain's Men had been bad
for business. Henslowe was too good a manager to lose an as-
set, however, and he leased out the Rose to Worcester's Men.

The Premiere of *Julius Caesar*

Julius Caesar was [William] Shakespeare's first Roman play, at-
tuned to the gaudy "classicism" of the Globe interior. A Roman setting, complete with marbled pillars, needed a Roman
play. The stage-directions for "*thunder*" and for "*thunder and
lightning*" also provided an opportunity to display the sound
effects of the new theatre. Unlike the extravagant playhouse,
however, the play itself is a triumph of simple diction and
chaste rhetoric; it is as if Shakespeare had somehow been able

to assume the Roman virtues and to adopt the Roman style. His deployment of forensic oratory is so skilled that it might have been composed by a classical rhetorician. He had the ability to blend himself with different states of man. In the very cadence and syntax of the words, he is Caesar. He exists within the formal periods of Brutus's prose and within the self-serving mellifluousness of Antony's verse.

The novelty of the new playhouse also aroused Shakespeare's ambitions, since in this play there is a more subtle sense of character, of motive, and of consequence. The emphasis is not so much upon event as upon personality. The action is so skilfully balanced that it becomes impossible to apportion praise or blame with any certainty. Is Brutus deluded or glorious? Is Caesar matchless or fundamentally flawed? Shakespeare seems almost deliberately to have established a new kind of protagonist, whose character is not immediately apparent or transparent to the audience. Shakespeare always finds it difficult to defend those things towards which he is most sympathetic, and in this particular play the distrust of the new is matched only by scepticism about the old. It is a play of oppositions and of contrasts in which there is no final resolution. In this same spirit it can be seen as a history play or as a revenge tragedy, or as both combined. It is a new kind of drama. He knows the sources, [contemporary English translator Thomas] North's translation of [ancient Greek and Roman historian] Plutarch principal among them, but he changes their emphasis and direction. He invents Caesar's deafness, too, as well as the scene in which Brutus and his co-conspirators steep themselves in the murdered Caesar's blood. There were other Roman plays in the period, written by Shakespeare's contemporaries, but they were content to give the historical narratives a spectacular and theatrical decoration. Shakespeare goes to the heart of the matter.

[English playwright] Ben Jonson resented its production, not least since it came from the pen of a man who had "little

William Shakespeare's play Julius Caesar *appeared on the stage of the Globe Theatre (pictured) on the theater's opening day.* © travellib europe/Alamy.

Latin." Jonson's play, *Every Man out of His Humour,* was performed later in the same year and within it are references to *Julius Caesar* which may be construed as playful or sarcastic. At one point the dying fall of "*Et tu, Brute!*" is satirised; this in itself is a clear indication that the original phrase was now known to playgoers. Among Shakespeare's audience in 1599 were two young men who knew very well the nature of betrayal. A letter of the period reveals that "my Lord Southampton and Lord Rutland come not to the Court. . . . They pass away the tyme in London merely in going to plaies every day."

A Preoccupation with Rulers

There is a reference to *Julius Caesar* in [Shakespeare's] *Henry V*, which was composed a few months after. . . . The English History [play] is just as much an exercise in ambiguity, in opposition and contrast, as *Julius Caesar*; but it is screwed to an even higher pitch. Is Henry a bullying thug or a great leader of men? Is he made of valour or formed from ice and snow? Is he an image of authority or a figure fit for ridicule? The scenes of military prowess and achievement are framed by a comic plot that subtly deflates this heroic tale of success. The king's speech beginning "Once more vnto the Breach, deare friends . . ." is immediately succeeded by the braggart Bardolph's "On, on, on, on, on, to the breach. . . ." The burlesque may not have been deliberate. Shakespeare did not have to stop and think about it. He did it naturally and instinctively. It was as inevitable as a pianist using both the black and the white keys.

On the character and motives of the king, black or white, it is possible that Shakespeare himself was not sure. But, clothed in the shimmering veil of Henry's rhetoric, they do not matter; Shakespeare was entranced by the idea of magnificence, and there is nothing like the exercise of power to create memorable lines and powerful scenes. . . .

Henry V is in fact the culmination of Shakespeare's preoccupation with kingship. Shakespeare invented the role of the player king. Certainly, more than any other dramatist before or since, he popularised the role of sovereign and managed infinitely to extend its range, while the imagery of the player king is unique to him. In his history plays, of course, the part of the monarch is the most significant and effective on the stage; but there are also Lear, Macbeth, Duncan, Claudius, Ferdinand, Cymbeline, Leontes and a host of noble rulers [from Shakespeare's tragic and romantic plays]. He uses the word "crown" 380 times, and Edmond Malone [Irish scholar and editor of Shakespeare's plays] commented perceptively that "when he means to represent any quality of the mind as eminently perfect, he furnishes the imaginary being whom he personifies, with a crown." One of his abiding images is that of the king as sun and, in his dramaturgy, he loves what is stately and what is grand. He was concerned with tragic narratives only in so far as they were concerned with persons of high degree; tragedies of "low life," which were written in this period, held no interest for him. But kings appear in his com-

edies as well as in his tragedies. They may not always be portrayed in a flattering light, but nevertheless he evinces collabo-
rative sympathy with them. It is notable that in his tragedies
the person of highest rank speaks the last lines of the play,
and in his later comedies it is always the king or principal
nobleman who pronounces the verdict upon what might be
called the final state of play. There is a prince in the conclud-
ing scene of thirteen out of his sixteen comedies.

It should not be forgotten that throughout his career he
was a regular receiver of court favours and that in the latter
part of his life he wore the royal livery as the king's true
servant. . . .

Shakespeare Playing the Ruler

He was possessed, or obsessed, by the inwardness of the ruler
rather than the ruled. The role of monarch seems to spring
naturally and instinctively from his imagination, and one
close student of Shakespeare's imagery has pointed out "how
continually he associates dreaming with kingship." Did he enjoy fantasies and day-dreams of power? There is indeed a
natural consonance between the player and the king, both
dressed in robes of magnificence and both obliged to play a
part. It may have been one reason why Shakespeare was attracted to the profession of acting in the first place.

Among his contemporaries he was well known for playing
kingly parts upon the stage. In 1610 [poet] John Davies wrote
a set of verses to "our English Terence, Mr. Will Shake-speare"
in which he declared that

Some say (good Will) which I, in sport, do
sing,

Had'st thou not plaid some Kingly parts in
sport,

Thou hadst bin a companion for a King.

The assumption seems to be that his manners would have been gracious and "gentle" enough to enjoy high companionship, had it not been for the fact that he was an actor. In another poem the same author considered that "the *stage* doth staine pure gentle *bloud*." In *Measure for Measure* there is an implicit comparison between the powers of the playwright and the power of the ruler of Vienna, guiding and moving human affairs from a distance.

Shakespeare did indeed play "kingly parts." It is surmised that he played Henry VI in the trilogy of that name, and Richard II against Burbage's Bolingbroke. Long theatrical tradition maintains that he played the ghost of the dead king in *Hamlet*, and that he might have doubled as the usurping king. The assumption of these parts was no doubt the result of an instinctive grace and authority, deepened by the theatrical assumption of *gravitas* [seriousness], but it may also be evidence of some natural predilection. He had a noble bearing and a graceful manner. Yet, somewhere within him, there is always [a] voice . . . mocking the king.

Social Issues in Literature

CHAPTER 2

Tyranny in Shakespeare's *Julius Caesar*

Julius Caesar Relies on Ancient Rome's Complex Political Stage

Coppelia Kahn

Coppelia Kahn, professor of English at Brown University, is the author of Man's Estate: Masculine Identity in Shakespeare.

In this viewpoint Kahn begins by providing the reader with a sketch of Roman history: the origin of Rome, the rule of the Tarquin kings and their expulsion, and the establishment of the Republic. Kahn then reveals that the very Republic the conspirators claim to defend in Julius Caesar *never really existed. Caesar gains power by denouncing rule by one man, and this complex, contradictory relationship undermines the purpose of the Republic. The Republican ideology and those who champion it are blind to the reality of Roman politics. Furthermore, unlike most critics, Kahn argues that Caesar and Brutus are much alike; both publicly advertise their support for a republic while privately believing just the opposite.*

When Cassius tries to persuade his friend Brutus that they must halt Julius Caesar's rise to power, Cassius speaks of an idealized "Rome" of the past in which kingship was unthinkable:

> Rome, thou hast lost the breed of noble
> bloods! . . .
>
> O, you and I have heard our fathers say
>
> There was a Brutus once that would have
> brooked

Th' eternal devil to keep his state in Rome

As easily as a king.

A few scenes later, Brutus wrestles with the question of whether Caesar intends to become king, and recalls his own namesake:

My ancestors did from the streets of Rome

The Tarquin drive when he was called a
king.

As many in [William] Shakespeare's audience might have known, Rome began as a kingship that lasted some 150 years until Lucius Junius Brutus, ancestor of this play's Brutus, led an uprising in 510 B.C. that drove the reigning dynasty from Rome, abolished kingship itself, and established the Roman Republic. Both Cassius and Brutus equate Rome with the Republic and the values it purports to embody. They see themselves as Romans because they believe in the Republic and because they repudiate kingship so that power can be shared among the elected rulers, the aristocratic patricians who make up the Senate, and the people. Then, supposedly, no one man can dominate Rome; all male citizens will be free, and equal. (The government of the United States, in which power is shared among the President, the Congress, and the Supreme Court, is modeled on the Roman Republic, and the pledge of allegiance to the flag mentions "the republic ... with liberty and justice for all.") Brutus, once he is convinced that Caesar "would be crowned," sees himself as destined to repeat his ancestor's heroic mission: by killing Caesar, he will, he thinks, restore the true "Rome"—the Republic.

The Vulnerable Republic

The Roman Republic, however, never existed in the pure form in which the conspirators imagine it, and the reign of terror unleashed by their assassination of Caesar gave rise precisely to the rule of "one man" that they hoped to prevent. Octavius Caesar became sole emperor of Rome by defeating the conspirators in the final battle at Philippi in 42 B.C. and then by conquering his former ally Antony at Actium in 31 B.C. This is the play's tragic irony, and some knowledge of Roman history can help us to appreciate it.

In the century or so preceding the assassination of Julius Caesar in 44 B.C., the Roman Republic endured almost constant upheavals. The reforms in land ownership introduced between 134 and 122 B.C. provoked fierce resistance from the patrician class, and those who introduced the reforms were killed after armed battles between their followers and those defending the Senate. The senators regained power for a time, but then two rival generals, Marius, in 107 B.C., and Sulla, in 88 B.C., took control. Each with his massive armies occupied Rome; each carried out a reign of terror—largely under republican law—in which his political opponents were openly slaughtered.

Next came Pompey, who acquired the surname *Magnus*, meaning "the great," by helping Sulla destroy Marius. (In the play's first scene, the tribunes recall Pompey as Julius Caesar's predecessor.) Granted extraordinary powers by the Senate, Pompey swept the Mediterranean clean of pirates and defeated Mithradates VI, king of Pontus, making himself in effect the uncrowned emperor of Rome's eastern provinces. Locked in rivalry with Julius Caesar, who defeated him at Pharsalus in 48 B.C., Pompey held more power and authority than any one man in Rome had ever had. The Republic never, for more than brief periods, functioned as it was supposed to—as a combination of monarchy (in the consuls), oligarchy (in the Senate), and democracy that, by keeping all three forms of power in balance, would prevent the worst tendencies of each. Instead, the Republic fostered the division of the aristocracy into factions and the rise of military superheroes whose armies were loyal to them rather than to the Republic.

The Myth of a Republic

The republican ideal that Cassius evokes to seduce Brutus into opposing Caesar, and that Brutus uses to justify murder, is closer to myth than to history (though it was also dearly cherished as an ideal even during the worst conflicts of the republican era). Or we might call it an ideology, which, according to [philosopher] Louis Althusser, is a set of imagined relations as opposed to the actual political conditions of Rome. Cassius correctly assumes that Brutus shares this ideology. As "noble bloods" of the ruling elite, both Cassius and Brutus believe themselves to have earned their reputations as "honorable men" by serving the state. That Caesar, one of their own class, has outstripped them in the ordinary course of advancement through state offices is an affront to their honor as Romans. Of course, Brutus and Cassius differ in character: Brutus wouldn't stoop to the deception Cassius practices by planting in Brutus' study faked petitions from citizens supposedly clamoring for Brutus to topple Caesar. And it wouldn't occur to Cassius to justify Caesar's murder by calling it "a sacrifice." Yet they are equally blinded to the complex politics of Rome by their shared republican mentality. *Julius Caesar* has often been treated almost as a set of individual character studies. And it is true that Shakespeare's "noble Romans" are vividly differentiated. However, they are all conceived within and motivated by a common sense of class identity as patricians and of national identity as Romans defending the Republic.

While Brutus and Cassius ponder their loss of status as Caesar's "underlings," within earshot a crowd roars for him. Though in person Caesar may fall short of the mystique he generates, he knows how to inspire massive public approval. In contrast, for Brutus and Cassius the people hardly exist. Casca's account of how Caesar refused the crown drips with aristocratic disdain for the "tag-rag people." Yet why, according to him, did the people cheer for Caesar?

... still as he refused [the crown] the rabblement hooted and clapped their chopped hands and threw up their sweaty nightcaps and uttered such a deal of stinking breath because Caesar refused the crown. ...

A Clash of Ideologies

Seemingly, the people too are captive to the republican ideal. Then Brutus' fear that "the people / Choose Caesar for their king" must be mistaken. Or is it? For when Caesar "perceived the common herd was glad he refused the crown, he plucked ... ope his doublet and offered them his throat to cut." He is obviously playing to the grandstands, in what amounts to a parody of serving "the general good," in order to milk the crowd's adoration. But does it lie within the people's power to confer the crown? Evidently not, for it is Antony who offers it, and in the next scene Casca says "the Senators tomorrow / Mean to establish Caesar as a king." The patricians, then, are divided into factions for and against Caesar. But is any faction strong enough to override the people's will? As Antony's funeral oration demonstrates, the man who can convince the masses that Caesar—in high republican fashion—was devoted to *them* can rule Rome. Thus it would appear that republican ideology can be successfully coopted by ambitious men like Caesar and Antony. While grasping power for their own interests, they convince those who give it to them that they use it only for "the general good"—thus establishing a set of imagined social relations that masks the real ones.

Brutus sets out to kill Caesar in the conviction that Caesar "would be crowned." The glimpses of Caesar that Shakespeare allows us neither confirm nor refute this belief. Grandiose but physically infirm, imperious but easily manipulated by flattery, in his last moments he resembles the Caesar of Casca's account who loves to delude himself and others into thinking that he embodies the selfless, constant servant of the state. "What touches us ourself shall be last served," he declares, and, refusing entreaties, continues:

But I am constant as the Northern Star,

Of whose true fixed and resting quality

There is no fellow in the firmament. . . .

Let me a little show it, even in this:

That I was constant Cimber should be banished

And constant do remain to keep him so.

Characterizations Mirror Rome's Complex Political Sphere

Disturbingly, it is Brutus who most resembles Caesar in playing the republican role. Both Caesar and Brutus are self-conscious about their particular virtues and concerned to display them publicly, no matter what their actual feelings. Caesar wants to be known for his courage. Warning Antony that Cassius' envy is dangerous, he says, "I rather tell thee what is to be feared / Than what I fear; for always I am Caesar." Alone with his wife, who urges him to heed the portents of disaster and stay home from the Capitol, he speaks of himself in the same ringing tones that mark his public utterance: "Caesar shall forth. The things that threatened me / Ne'er looked but on my back." Brutus, quite similarly, takes pains to make public the moral principles behind his actions. When he is alone, he calls the prospect of murdering Caesar "a dreadful thing" and refers to the "monstrous visage" of conspiracy. But once the conspiracy gathers, he refers only to the "virtue of our enterprise."

Julius Caesar Is the Tragedy of the Roman Republic

Andrew Hadfield

Andrew Hadfield, head of the English Department at the University of Sussex, is the author of Shakespeare and Republicanism.

In his introduction to an edition of Julius Caesar, *Hadfield poses the essential question in the play: Is Shakespeare more sympathetic with the forces of tyranny, represented in Caesar, or with the republicans' conspiracy against tyranny? After demonstrating Shakespeare's sympathies for each major character in turn, Hadfield proposes that the play is not a tragedy for any particular character but rather the tragic tale of the Roman Republic itself. Both politically and culturally, he argues, Rome was ready for change, and even the values and actions expected to strengthen the Republic ultimately undermined its very existence. Hadfield suggests that this dramatized condition of Rome may have caused Shakespeare's contemporary audience to look inward at their own unbalanced monarchy.*

*J*ulius Caesar is a pivotal play in [William] Shakespeare's career. Performed in 1599, it was probably the first play presented at the newly constructed Globe, a large, expensive theater that Shakespeare's company, the Lord Chamberlain's men, needed to fill. The play itself is tense and dramatic, and, while Shakespeare's audience would have already been familiar with the story, the play offers a fresh and compelling study of the destructive conflict of major historical actors undermined by their own limitations. Topical and allusive, Shakespeare's text dares the audience to make connections between the fall of the Roman Republic and their own times. The play ushered in a new, more mature and confident phase of Shakespeare's writing that saw him produce his major tragedies—*Hamlet, Othello, King Lear,* and *Macbeth*—in the next few years.

Julius Caesar shows Shakespeare finally realizing the potential that he had always shown throughout his early career. Few Shakespeare plays have been more frequently performed on stage in the last three centuries or studied in schools, demonstrating that what was clearly a successful and popular work in 1599 has captured audiences and readers ever since. Even people who have never seen or read the play can recite *"Et tu, Brutè?"* and "Friends, Romans, countrymen, lend me your ears." And, like many of the most celebrated literary works, *Julius Caesar* inspires controversy and occasionally conspiracy theories, with some readers even regarding the play as a religious allegory (Julius Caesar, after all, has the same initials as Jesus Christ) and the assassination of Caesar as a mythical event of cosmic significance.

Whose Side Does Shakespeare Take?

The question that has dominated critical interpretation has been which political faction Shakespeare represents with greater sympathy. Does he tilt toward the republicans, representing Brutus as the "noblest Roman of them all," as Antony declares him to be at the end of the play? Or does he recoil in horror at the dreadful act of violence at the heart of the play, showing us that the republican faction is a group of deluded revolutionaries who have murdered a great hero whose flaws are insubstantial? Perhaps the dominant mode of reading *Julius Caesar* has been to assume that Shakespeare is wisely commenting on the follies of human history, revealing to us that violence inevitably fails to reform corrupt government, only exaggerating the miseries of the suffering people who have had to live under a repressive regime.

There is much to recommend this reading, even if it conveniently reproduces the familiar idea that Shakespeare was a conservative figure who had an instinctive hatred of crowds and mob rule, frequently warning his audience and readers against the follies of premature, rash action. The play does suggest that Caesar is probably not the dreadful tyrant who has sometimes been portrayed, especially in productions that have sought to represent him as a fascist dictator. Caesar is feeble and ailing, deaf in one ear and lacking a robust physical presence, not a vigorous and driven ideologue. Dreadful crimes are committed in his name, such as the silencing of the tribunes, Murellus and Flavius, who object to the celebrations for his victories over Pompey, but they are not necessarily authorized by him. He is arrogant and naïve, especially when he refuses to listen to good advice, and he has little idea of how to govern those who surround him or, indeed what they are planning and how they might feel about him.

But, as Brutus admits in his orchard, Caesar has to be killed not because of what he has done but because of what he might do, logic that is problematic on a number of levels, not least because Caesar is hardly unformed. Nevertheless, even if he is no towering twentieth-century dictator, as he has often been represented in more recent productions of the play, Caesar is hardly a straightforwardly admirable character. The opening scene is a reminder that Caesar has achieved power through his triumph over his rival, Pompey, and that he has been prepared to fight a bloody and divisive civil war to rule in Rome. His ally, Mark Antony, delivers a superb funeral oration for his dead friend and leader, but is prepared to rip the social fabric of Rome apart for his own personal revenge.

Flaws of the Republican Conspirators

The republican faction is itself undeniably flawed, and only the most partisan reader could argue that Shakespeare nails his colors to their mast. Cassius is sly and underhanded, having enough knowledge of human behavior to flatter Brutus into joining his cause by throwing stones at Brutus's window and claiming that the people are demanding that Brutus act to save them. Even if Cassius's devoted, homoerotic regard for Brutus humanizes him in the last two acts as the republican forces are hunted down and destroyed, it is still hard not to feel that Cassius, like Mark Antony, allows personal loyalties to override any sense of allegiance to wider communities or feelings of responsibility toward other human beings whose fates he is able to control.

Brutus is undoubtedly a man of principle and constancy, yet he often behaves ridiculously. His speech justifying the assassination of Caesar is based on shaky premises and faulty logic. He delivers another flat speech when needing to persuade the people to support the actions of the conspirators, failing to make a series of specific points against Caesar (that his military background renders him incapable of appreciating the complex nature of Roman government, that he was prepared to wage a brutal civil war to get what he wanted) and concentrating instead on Caesar's abstract and hardly capital crime of "ambition." He is aloof and cold as both friend and husband, refusing to discuss matters with his intelligent and faithful wife who is prepared to wound and finally kill herself because of him, and then failing to see how crucial his alliance with Cassius is as their campaign becomes more and more desperate. Most important, his judgment is often simply wrong, and he is too arrogant to realize how foolish his actions are. He allows Antony to speak at Caesar's funeral against the sage advice of Cassius, who realizes Antony's ability to undermine their cause. He insists that they all bathe in Caesar's blood after they have killed Caesar as a sign of their commitment to "Peace, freedom, and liberty," a moment of grim comedy. And he insists on immediately engaging the army of the triumvirate when no prudent general would take such an absurd risk.

Brutus, as these character summaries indicate, is easily the most important figure in the play (Caesar, after all, dies in Act Three), and *Julius Caesar* has sometimes been read as his tragedy. However, we may wish to resist such efforts to see the play as the tragedy of a single heroic individual. Greek tragedy, and Aristotle's influential reading of the body of drama that defined European theater, emphasized that the action could carry the tragic effect rather than the audience needing to see one figure as a tragic hero. Shakespeare's play can be read as a comment on the tragic state of Rome as the city was in the painful process of transforming itself from a republic to an empire. The characters and their personalities matter less than the situations that they find themselves in and the limited solutions at their disposal.

From Monarchy to Republic to Empire

Roman history was taught in all Elizabethan schools, and everyone who had had an education—and many who had not—knew the basic history of the ancient city-state, knowledge that cannot be taken for granted today. Roman history was widely believed to be cyclical in nature. Rome was traditionally thought to have been founded by its first king, Romulus, who killed his brother Remus after a quarrel. A series of dynasties ruled Rome until the Tarquins, the last kings of Rome, assumed control. Their rule ended when Tarquinus Sextus, the son of the tyrannical king Tarquinus Superbus, raped the chaste Roman matron Lucrece, as Shakespeare narrated in his own version of the story, *The Rape of Lucrece* (1594). Unable to live with her shame, Lucrece killed herself, and the angry Romans, led by Brutus's ancestor, Lucius Junius Brutus, rose up and exiled the Tarquins, vowing never to be ruled by kings again. In place of the monarchy, they established the Roman Republic, a stable form or state that treated all citizens relatively equally, trusting the senators who met in the Capitol building to determine how the city should be governed in consultation with other officials such as the tribunes (elected by the plebeians to represent them).

The Republic was a remarkably successful institution, working through a series of checks and balances to chart a middle course against extremes. Nonetheless, it came under severe pressure as Rome expanded into an empire, in part because it now had to govern vast areas that were hard to control and in part because the army became an increasingly powerful element of Roman society that sought more control for itself. The Republic began to degenerate as feuding factions of generals, inflated by their own triumphs, threatened the fabric of government. Pompey the Great clashed with Julius Caesar, the latter triumphing and becoming dictator. Although Caesar was then assassinated, a series of bloody civil wars erupted throughout the empire until Octavius stood alone as sole ruler of Rome, crowning himself as its first emperor, Augustus. His reign was controversial, having been supported and condemned in equal measure by subsequent historians. But he was followed by some of the most brutal dictators in world history: the infamous Tiberius, Caligula, and Nero. During their reigns, many of the works that the Elizabethans studied were written, including the influential histories by [Roman historians] Tacitus and Livy as well as the republican anti-epic by [Roman poet] Lucan, the *Pharsalia*. It is little wonder that the legacy of the Republic was regarded with much more enthusiasm than that of the vicious early days of the Empire.

As this brief overview suggests, Roman history seemed straightforward and easy to remember, and readers were encouraged to make comparisons with events in their own times. Early audiences of *Julius Caesar* were clearly in a position to make such connections when they saw the play, given the ubiquity of Roman history and the wealth of comparisons made between the history of Rome and the history of England by Shakespeare's contemporaries. The Rome we see represented on stage in Shakespeare's play is a frightened, paranoid, and vicious place in which individuals find that they can trust no one outside a select circle of close friends because there are no public institutions left to support debate and proper government. The city Shakespeare depicts bears little comparison to that of the Republic at its most stable, when Rome was famed for public oratory and political debate. While the Republic staged great trials of miscreants in which famed orators argued the merits of cases and political decisions were openly debated by all citizens, in *Julius Caesar* individuals hide in corners planning violent acts of desperation. A more pointed contrast still is that between Brutus the founder of the Roman Republic and Brutus the assassin. While the actions of the first Brutus do actually lead to "Peace, freedom, and liberty," those of the second, despite the rallying cry, lead only to chaos and civil war, the death of the incumbent ruler only leading to more deaths.

Time Out of Joint

We must not, however, blame this failure to live up to the ideals of the Republic simply on the characters in Shakespeare's play. A companion piece to *Julius Caesar* is *Hamlet*, another drama centered on a political assassination in which the frustrated and doomed hero exclaims, "The time is out of joint. O cursed spite, / That ever I was born to set it right." Hamlet realizes the weight of the unwelcome burden that has been thrust upon him and which he would never have chosen himself. The same dilemma confronts the characters in *Julius Caesar*, especially Brutus. That he fails to reproduce the results of his predecessor and namesake suggests that when history does repeat itself it is invariably a pale shadow or a parody of what went before. The time waste ripe for the transformation of Rome when the Tarquins ruled. They were genuine tyrants who needed to be overthrown, and there was a popular will that meant that the Republic became a realizable possibility.

Julius Caesar is only a potential tyrant, not obviously worse than those men who surround him, and the popular will for the revitalization of the Republic is faked by Cassius. Far from exhibiting a union of leaders and populace, the play shows the conspirators huddling in small groups nervously making grand plans while the people celebrate the achievements of Caesar and ignore the attempts of the tribunes to stir up sympathy for the Republic. As in *Hamlet*, the time is out of joint, and things cannot be put right.

The Republic was able to function so well in the first place because of two central features. One of these was the esteem in which Romans regarded eloquence in speech and writing, including eloquence in political speech, forensic oratory, forms of praise, treatises, letters, works of fiction, and dialogues. The second was the value Romans placed upon friendship, which bound citizens together in a common enterprise. We see eloquence go badly awry in *Julius Caesar*. Caesar himself makes no important speech and concentrates instead on oracular pronouncements that are invariably bizarre and reveal more about his own sense of his self-worth than about anything in the world beyond his ego, a worrying but all too familiar tendency of the isolated dictator. He frequently refers to himself in the third person, as though he had already become a god (an obsession of later Roman emperors). When Calphurnia does manage to persuade him—albeit briefly—that he ought not attend the Senate on the Ides of March, he informs Decius, who has come to collect him, that he will not falsely claim to be sick:

Shall Caesar send a lie?

Have I in conquest stretched mine arm so far

To be afeard to tell graybeards the truth?

Decius, go tell them Caesar will not come

Decius asks for a cause to be given so that he can avoid humiliation but is told that the cause is simply Caesar's will. And yet, as we all know, Caesar is eventually persuaded to attend when a more flattering interpretation is given of his wife's frightening dream.

Such words hardly resemble the achievements of the Roman Republic in its heyday represented for Elizabethans mainly by the works of Cicero, the eloquent and outspoken conscience of the Republic. Cicero produced a whole library of important works, including dialogues, orations made in the Senate and in famous trials, and treatises, most famously on the duties of a citizen, the value of friendship, and the elements of the republican constitution. Cicero was a master of the art of rhetoric, able to tailor any argument to an appropriate form in order to persuade an audience of his position, whether praising great men, prosecuting wrongdoers, or reminding citizens of their loyalty to their country. Cicero does indeed appear in Shakespeare's play, but only as a minor figure. Cicero appears in the third scene of the play, during the great storm onset of the action once the conspirators have made their decision to kill Caesar. Like Caesar—but for different reasons—he says little, in contrast to the known record of his loquaciousness and ability to manipulate words better than anyone else. Cicero refuses to join the conspirators and appears a calm presence in contrast to the intensely nervous Casca. We eventually learn that he has been put to death. Nonetheless, Cicero's reputation and his role in promoting the virtues of republican Rome cast a shadow over the action of the play. The fact that he has little chance to speak or act in *Julius Caesar* is a potent sign that his values cannot flourish in the cloak-and-dagger world of the play; the eloquent speech and writing that Rome at its best produced and promoted are now irrelevant. Cicero may disparage the claims of the conspirators as well as the actions of Caesar, and stand above the superstition and chaos that envelop Rome, but he is powerless to change the course of the city's destiny.

The Republic Is Destroyed from Within

It is a sad fact that republicans such as Brutus are poor orators—partly because they have no investment in or experience of trying to persuade an audience of citizens that they are right—whereas their most significant opponent, Mark Antony, is a brilliant orator, attentive to the needs and demands of the situation, fully in command of his material, and sensitive to what his audience wants to hear. There is, of course, considerable irony in the fact that Antony is able to derail the republican cause using its own traditional virtues. Not only does he demonstrate that he is a more eloquent speaker than any of his opponents, but he also does what he does for the sake of his dead friend, Julius Caesar. The tables are neatly turned, a further sign of the times when nothing stays in one place. The irony multiplies when, in *Antony and Cleopatra* (1606), Antony meets a similar fate as he dies fighting his erstwhile allies while the Roman Republic implodes from within.

Antony's touching but dangerous loyalty to Caesar is balanced by the friendship between Cassius and Brutus. We witness a world in which the virtues of friendship should lead to stronger ties that enhance and bond the social fabric of the state, but, in fact, here they help to undermine it. Cassius's highly charged love for Brutus helps to persuade him to hatch the plot to assassinate Caesar, a telling example of virtue turned to vice, while Brutus's love for Cassius leads him consistently into terrible errors of judgment. At the end of the play Antony praises Brutus as the "noblest Roman of them all," excusing him from acting against Caesar out of impure motives, unlike his allies, who he argues acted out of "envy of great Caesar." Antony has missed what is obvious to the audience: just as he acted out of love for Caesar—and was prepared to countenance virtually any consequence to avenge his dead friend—so did Cassius act out of his devotion to Brutus as well as his hatred of Caesar. The two friendships serve to destroy the Republic, the very state that encouraged men to develop such relationships with each other, another keen irony that shadows the play.

The most eagerly anticipated scene in the play for much of its stage history was the quarrel between Brutus and Cassius in Act Four, scene three. Here we see the two doomed generals talking at cross purposes and revealing a breach that can never be healed, one that fatally undermines their military strategy. Cassius and Brutus have vastly different values. Cassius values his friendship with Brutus before all else, so much so that he wants Brutus's regard for him to obscure any sense of Cassius's human flaws. Brutus, in contrast, wants Cassius to adhere to an absolute scale of moral values that no one but the "noblest Roman of them all" could possibly achieve. Their division is not only a pitiful human tragedy, one of the many contained in this remarkable play, but an indication of the collapse of generally accepted values that characterizes the fall of the Roman Republic.

The Danger of Roman and English Tyranny

Julius Caesar is a splendid play: complicated, controversial, full of intense dramatic moments, and eloquent even when lack of eloquence is represented on stage. Shakespeare clearly wanted his audience to make connections between the events that finally destroyed the Roman Republic and the impending death of Tudor England. Was England descending into chaos with the absence of a proper central authority, as Elizabeth grew ever older and, according to many of her subjects, remote from the needs and desires of the people she governed? Were her chief courtiers acting like the Roman senators who eventually decided to assassinate their leader, even if they would never dare to commit such a sacrilegious act? Would her death plunge the land into a civil war like the one that had torn Rome apart? Of course, this is not to insist that all readers and audiences bear such connections in mind each time they experience the play. *Julius Caesar* is a tragedy that cannot be limited to the interests and anxieties that surrounded its first production. As Shakespeare's best-known Roman play, it has inspired a range of creative interpretations, and the dangers of unchecked tyranny, like those of self-deceived would-be saviors, are known in every age. Nevertheless, understanding the Roman history that Shakespeare imaginatively recreates enables us to appreciate the significance, range, and depth of the meanings of the play.

Shakespeare Defines the Elizabethan Aristocratic Identity

Wayne A. Rebhorn

Wayne A. Rebhorn is a literature professor at the University of Texas and the author of Renaissance Debates on Rhetoric.

In this selection Rebhorn's study of Julius Caesar *centers on the Roman aristocracy, who claim to revolt against tyranny. The point of the play's class politics, he argues, is not the aristocracy's ideological objection to a monarchy or tyranny but rather the objection to one of their own class, Caesar, who is exceeding the powers of the rest. Rebhorn uses the word* emulation *to describe the relationships among members of the aristocracy who no longer seek to serve their country but prefer to promote the shared aristocratic identity. This upper class in Rome mirrors the aristocracy in Elizabethan England. Their ambition is not for a country with representational government free of tyranny; their desire is simply to maintain and grow their power. They are recognizable not only by their social standing but also by the way they attempt to surpass one another as gentlemen.*

In the late summer or autumn of 1599 ... [William] Shakespeare's company brought to the stage the tragedy of *Julius Caesar*. Although it is often read as a play about the killing of a king and expressing a real ambivalence on that score, it would be equally productive to see it as depicting a struggle among aristocrats—senators—aimed at preventing one of their number from transcending his place and destroying the

Wayne A. Rebhorn, "The Crisis of the Aristocracy in *Julius Caesar*," *Renaissance Quarterly*, vol. 43, no. 1, Spring 1990, pp. 78–85, 106–109. Copyright © 1990 by Renaissance Quarterly, published by University of Chicago. Reproduced by permission of the author and publisher.

system in which they all ruled as a class. In this perspective, then, the assassination is not regicide, but an attempt to restore the status quo ante. The conspirators strike down an individual, Julius Caesar, whose behavior displays and is characterized in terms that could not help but suggest emulation to an Elizabethan. However, the assassination is carried out by individuals whose actions are presented in the play in exactly the same way. In other words, although the motives of the conspirators, and especially those of Brutus, must be distinguished from Caesar's as well as Antony's and Octavius' in many respects, all are nevertheless animated by the same fundamental drive, the drive to excel all others, to "out-imitate" their fellows.

All the Roman senators can thus be read as versions of the same basic character type. Critics have, for instance, commented on the way that *Julius Caesar* actively deconstructs the opposition between Brutus and Caesar which it simultaneously seems to insist upon: although it invites the spectator to separate the "gentle" Brutus from the pompous Caesar who repeatedly speaks of himself in the third person, it simultaneously yokes the two men together, distinguishing them from all the other characters in the play both by virtue of their similar situations—both have wives and are seen in domestic settings—and, more important, by virtue of their shared character traits: an intolerance of others' opinions, a susceptibility to flattery, an overweening self-confidence. Such similarities have been used to qualify Brutus' status as the hero of the play, to identify moral failings in him that constitute his "tragic flaw." I would argue that the play not only undermines—without cancelling—the differences between Brutus and Caesar, but, more important, as it links the pair together, it stresses their resemblances to all the other aristocrats as well and identifies emulation as the common denominator of the entire group.

The Problem of Aristocratic Identity

I would argue that if the play presents the characters and values of Brutus, Cassius, and the others to create an image of ancient Roman civilization, it simultaneously holds "the mirror up to nature" in Shakespeare's own world, showing "the very age and body of the time his form and pressure." Just as Hamlet feels a play about a murder in Vienna has application to the world of Denmark, so Elizabethans in general read literature and history with an eye to their topical interest, their application to the present.... [It] is reasonable to infer that Elizabethans coming to *Julius Caesar* would have seen in the play not just a re-creation of the revered Roman past but a representation of aspects of their contemporary social and political order.

What they would have seen in particular in the play, thanks to the parallels created among Brutus, Cassius, and the rest, is the presentation of the Roman aristocracy as a distinct class that is remarkably similar to the Elizabethan aristocracy and that is defined and defines itself in two basic ways. First, it does so by distinguishing itself from those who are not aristocrats, from the plebeians, who are rebuked by the Tribunes as "blocks" and "stones" and disparaged by Casca as "rabblement." But the aristocrats are also defined in the play by emulation; they are recognizable not merely because they enjoy a particular position in the social order relative to other groups, but because they possess a shared "character." Such a concern with aristocratic self-definition was of vital interest in Elizabethan culture and was in good measure the result of the dislocations caused by social mobility and the ontological insecurity that mobility produced for Englishmen used to living in a seemingly immutable, intensely hierarchical society. Aristocratic identity was a problem, and writers responded to it with a vast outpouring of courtesy books, poetry, essays, and even epics such as *The Faerie Queene* [by English poet Edmund Spenser], all concerned with the fashioning—and hence

Wayne A. Rebhorn believes the upper class of Rome depicted in Shakespeare's play Julius Caesar *(pictured in a performance at Stratford, Ontario) reflected the aristocracy in Elizabethan England.* The Stratford Festival. Reproduced by permission.

the defining—of the gentleman or the nobleman. These works all participated in the large-scale cultural project of defining aristocratic behavior and values and distinguishing them from what characterized commoners, just as royal proclamations, for instance, tried to impose such distinctions by means of sumptuary restrictions. Thus they sought, in different ways, to reconfirm some version of the stratified, hierarchical social order described by political writers. *Julius Caesar*, of course, shares Elizabethans' concern to define aristocratic identity....

The historical context to which *Julius Caesar* refers, then, is both a mass of texts concerned with defining aristocratic behavior and values, and actual gentlemen and aristocrats, many of whom read those texts and to whom those texts referred. Moreover, the relation between the play and this context is far from simple. The play may be said to reflect its con-

text insofar as it is seen as merely presenting the preoccupations of many of Shakespeare's contemporaries. But at the
same time, it also participates in the constitution of that context: it defines the shape of Elizabethans' preoccupations for
them, in a sense supplying the very language they needed to
articulate their fears and desires. In other words, *Julius Caesar*,
like any text, is not a *repetition* of its context, but a *representation* of it; it does not simply reiterate what is already
known but re-forms it, thereby actually helping to constitute
the very context of which it is a part. It is not a mirror but a
shaping presence. What is more, as a shaping presence, as a
re-presentation, the play must be recognized as having an active, rather than a passive, merely reflective, relation to what it
represents as well as to the audience viewing that representation: that is, the play offers a particular perspective on its context, seeking both to define the shape of what it represents
and to shape its audience's response to that representation.
Consequently, I shall argue that *Julius Caesar*, although certainly voicing—and hence repeating—its culture's concern
with aristocratic identity, goes beyond mere reiteration by defining and clarifying that concern and by articulating its own,
distinctive point of view on the problem. . . .

Competition Among the Aristocracy

The central value that directs the behavior of all the aristocrats in *Julius Caesar* is emulation in the several, contradictory
senses of that word. To focus on one of its aspects: the emulation they all feel appears in the form of their omnipresent rivalry with one another, in their competition for preeminence,
in their factionalism that leads to assassination and civil strife.
Emulation is explicitly identified as the primary motive behind their slaying of Julius Caesar whose "virtue," according to
the minor character Artemidorus who tries to warn him of
the conspiracy, "cannot live / Out of the teeth of emulation."
Because of his famous "lean and hungry look," Cassius seems

the perfect embodiment of this quality, but as he recounts his "history" of the swimming match with Julius Caesar in the second scene of the play, he reveals that Caesar, who initially proposed the contest, is fully as emulous as he. When Cassius bests his opponent, he winds up carrying the exhausted Caesar on his shoulders in a gesture that he compares to that of the archetypal Roman, Aeneas, carrying his father out of Troy.... Here, although Cassius uses it for purposes of self-celebration, Shakespeare employs it ironically as indicating the triumph of one man over another, not as humble service to an acknowledged superior and moral authority. This "history" thus reveals that Julius Caesar is certainly right in being wary of Cassius because of his "lean and hungry" look, but it also reveals that what Julius Caesar sees in Cassius is at least in part a projection of qualities he himself possesses.

Cassius' behavior in "saving" Caesar typifies the play's conception of heroism that no longer means the service to the "patria" for which "pius Aeneas" was known from antiquity to the Renaissance. Rather, heroism has degenerated into competition *within* the patria, as the members of the ruling class jockey for positions of dominance over their fellows. Significantly, the Roman senators in *Julius Caesar* are presented as participating in a political struggle rather than military conquest directed at a common enemy or aiming to extend the bounds of the empire. Even Caesar is characterized in terms of his rivalry with other senators rather than as the conqueror of the Gauls or the Britons. Indeed, there is virtually no mention in the play of his past victories or triumphs; instead, the stress falls on his present physical weaknesses and other defects: his epileptic fainting fit at the stadium, his deafness in one ear, perhaps even his superstitiousness. Moreover, not only does *Julius Caesar* reveal that the Roman aristocrats no longer seek to serve the interests of the patria, but it suggests that their behavior, which is still defined in ideal terms as that of warriors and heroes, actually opposes them to it. The emulation at the roots of their being pits them against each other in destructive, internecine combat, and it generates contests, such as the swimming match Caesar proposed to Cassius, which needlessly expose them to danger and even destruction and which serve no military end whatsoever. Such contests are willful, gratuitous forms of risk-taking that purchase identity at the price of potential personal extinction and that are carried forward without a thought for the good of the state. Indeed, so little do these Roman aristocrats resemble "pius Aeneas" that they seem much more like his opponents or like those defective heroes in the *Aeneid*, Nisus and Euryalus, whose willful pursuit of personal glory interferes with service to the patria and leads to their deaths.

Shakespeare's aristocrats in *Julius Caesar* share a conception of identity which might well be called that of the "imperial self." They possess an urge to personal aggrandizement, a will to extend the terrain of the self until it entirely dominates the human landscape, like the Colossus Caesar under whose giant legs Cassius claims he and his fellow aristocrats, "petty men," walk about in search of graves. . . .

The Aristocrats' Imperial Will

In the fifteenth and early sixteenth centuries, the aristocracy was a class of feudal magnates who defined themselves primarily as warriors, commanded troops of loyal retainers and dependents, and enjoyed considerable power in the country. Over the next one hundred years or so, because of the efforts of ever more absolutist monarchs to concentrate power in their own hands, the aristocracy became a class of courtiers who often had little or no military experience and who exercised power primarily insofar as those monarchs were willing to grant it to them. These courtiers were placed in often desperate financial straits by the general price rise in the period and by the enormous expenses of life at court and in London, and they became increasingly dependent for honors and financial rewards on kings and queens whose resources, no matter how freely given, were never able to satisfy them sufficiently. Spending more and more of their time in the city away from their estates, they alienated the peasants on those estates, especially after the accession of James I, by jacking up rents in order to meet expenses, and they became associated with courts whose licentiousness scandalized the populace generally and especially that part of it inclined towards Puritanism. Gradually, the aristocracy lost so much of its prestige and influence that, on the eve of the Civil War, it was totally unable to control elections to Parliament as it normally did. . . .

Julius Caesar depicts a sick world in the process of succumbing to centralized, absolutist, one-man rule not because of the exceptional talents of characters such as Caesar and Octavius, but because of the emulation, the imperial will, which animates the behavior of the entire class of aristocrats and leads ineluctably to their unintended, collective self-destruction. Driven by the hunger of emulation to extend endlessly the terrain of the self, they destroy and will keep destroying one another until the stage is bare and only a single imperial will is left. As a character in another play [Shakespeare's *Troilus and Cressida*], a play also concerned with emulation and factionalism, sums it up with fitting finality: the appetite driving them on is "an universal wolf"; it will "make perforce an universal prey / And last eat up himself."

Julius Caesar Presents the Anarchy-Tyranny Dilemma as Inevitable

William Rosen and Barbara Rosen

William Rosen was a professor of English at the University of Connecticut and the author of Shakespeare and the Craft of Tragedy. *Barbara Rosen coedited the Signet Classic Edition of* Julius Caesar *with William Rosen.*

In the following viewpoint, William and Barbara Rosen argue that Shakespeare's Julius Caesar *was informed by the specter of political instability in the playwright's own country. They point out that when Shakespeare wrote the play, there was a gnawing fear in England about what would happen when the aging and childless Queen Elizabeth died. Historically, Rome faced either a tyranny or a republic, but the authors state that in* Julius Caesar *the playwright presents a new dichotomy: tyranny versus anarchy.*

When *Julius Caesar* was performed in 1599, Elizabethans must have seen in its events their own uncertainties about a sudden change of rule and its possible consequences. Elizabeth was over sixty-five; a painted old woman living on a parody of flattery that had once been sincere. Her subjects knew that she was beginning to fail, but they had no idea of what was to come next, for there was no heir, and the Queen would name none. Once again there might be a disputed succession, the overriding dread of the time. It is striking that [William] Shakespeare, turning from *Henry V* (1599), began to write not the "history" but the "tragedy" of *Julius Caesar*,

William and Barbara Rosen, "The Specialty of Rule," *Twentieth Century Interpretations of Julius Caesar: A Collection of Critical Essays,* ed. Leonard F. Dean. Reprinted with the permission of Simon & Schuster, Inc. Copyright © 1968 Prentice-Hall, Inc. All rights reserved.

perhaps finding in the civil wars that followed the death of an aging ruler some reflections of the horrors that could overtake his own country, and seeing in the complexities of a power struggle the problems for his own government.

The Fickle Mob Mentality

The beginning of *Julius Caesar* shows the fickleness of popular opinion: the citizens are celebrating the triumph of Caesar, whereas only a short time before they wholeheartedly supported Pompey. Having overcome and slain Pompey, Caesar rides high on the Wheel of Fortune; but as the action progresses, the populace shifts allegiances with shifting fortunes. When Brutus speaks after the death of Caesar, the response is: "Let him be Caesar." After hearing Antony speak, the people switch their affection to "noble Antony," and want to "burn the house of Brutus." In the historical story of Julius Caesar the issue is between two forms of government, absolute monarchy and a republic. But the concept of a republic was alien to Elizabethan England, and Shakespeare utterly discounts either its possibility or desirability in his play. Departing from [ancient Greek and Roman historian] Plutarch, his main source, he makes the central characters much more surely in command of events than in fact they were. The Roman Senate, with its system of debate and voting, is left completely out of the picture; we get, instead, a subservient Parliament as background for the conspirators. Not particularly interested in the intricacies of Roman politics, Shakespeare concentrates on the ability of various leaders to hold power; less concerned with heroes and villains than with styles of public life that demonstrate qualities of leadership, he shows how men act, and how they are then forced to contend with the unexpected results of action.

The unexpected shifts in political action often require that strategies of public policy have a kind of moral flexibility which appears as mere opportunism in private life. Elizabeth's policy, for example, was so pragmatic that it is impossible to discover in its workings her personal beliefs. She used paid informers, spies, and *agents provocateurs*. The graceless convolutions of her policy kept Europe guessing; her meanness drove her most faithful public servants into debt and despair. Yet few doubted that her most squalid devices were subordinate to an extraordinary sense of statesmanship. The necessary was always done, though seldom elegantly or morally; the results of action were always dealt with on their own merits.

The Complexity of Rule

Because the royal position was unchallengeable in Elizabethan thinking about the nature of things, the King could act without regard to personal advancement; his least pleasing acts could therefore be free of self-interest. In *Richard II*, however, we see the problem of the "evil" king; there is a discrepancy between the office and the man who fills it, and yet, no matter how bad the king, rebellion can never be excused: it may seem essential, but it is, at best, a "necessary evil" for which the revolutionary, like a Greek tragic hero, incurs guilt and punishment. Henry IV can never wear Richard's crown in peace. Plagued by rebellion, and tormented by the thought that his son, Hal, is not only unworthy, but ambitious for the crown, he accepts his troubles as divine punishment for his own rebellion against Richard. His death, he tells his son, will remove the curse from the crown, "for what in me was purchased / Falls upon thee in a more fairer sort, / So thou the garland wear'st successively." As Henry V could succeed to rule without sin, but not his father, who won the throne by eliminating a legitimate ruler, so Octavius can succeed, but not the conspirators.

Because there is no kingship in *Julius Caesar* and God has therefore no representative in the system of government, Fortune (in public affairs) is not bound to the service of divine order, and her changes are everywhere apparent. There are not many plays in which events are so patently determined by slight miscalculations, mistakes of judgment, wrong "hunches," flawless logic applied to the wrong problem, or misplaced outbreaks of emotion warping decisions. Intention is continually frustrated by event. Actions produce results that are quite different from the ones which had been planned. It is possible that Plutarch's narrative technique provides another explanation for the emotional ambivalence of *Julius Caesar* (as well as Shakespeare's other Roman plays). In striving for fullness and accuracy of assessment, Plutarch shifts from a favorable account of a character's traits and actions to an unfavorable point of view and back again with a startling abruptness, and usually refuses a final judgment. We are left with a number of viewpoints or . . . with a collection of likenesses and differences that often lead to a curious kind of double vision, particularly in the comparisons of one character with another.

Our estimation of the characters and events of *Julius Caesar* is liable to shift according to our viewpoint: if we react according to our personal sympathies, Brutus is more likable than a superstitious, vain Caesar; if we consider public consequences, Brutus is far less commendable because he brings to Rome chaos and injustice, not "Peace, freedom, and liberty!" He kills only a man, not the spirit of Caesar, which comes back to haunt him at Sardis and Philippi, and finally to triumph, in the person of Octavius Caesar.

Judging Candidates for Leadership in *Julius Caesar*

The play demands more than a partial response; it asks that we judge a man not only for what he is but what he does. Consequences are no less important than intentions; we see that well-meaning is no guarantee of well-doing, and that bad things done for a good cause, or by people who think themselves good, are still bad. But not to do the bad things which government sometimes requires is also disastrous—witness the public failures of Brutus. Although virtue guides the civilized conduct of individuals, in this play the shifting concerns of public action, governed by necessity, demand more pragmatic laws. There are no easy solutions to the dilemmas and ironies that result.

Caesar shows great strength as the "constant," disinterested ruler who will not give in to the private entreaties of an Artemidorus or Cimber; he is also superstitious, and can be led by flattery. Both implacability and weakness contribute to his downfall. The envious Cassius belittles Caesar for not being as physically strong as he, yet in the practical matters of power politics he is emotionally unable to stand against Brutus, of whose moral qualities he is in awe. Brutus can kill Caesar to prevent tyranny, yet he cannot safeguard the deed by eliminating Antony as well, nor can he strengthen his cause by resorting to forced loans to finance his army. . . . Antony, in contrast, brilliantly uses every political trick there is, and can barter human lives without a qualm. Yet he genuinely lacks ambition; his aim is simple revenge for Caesar's death, and nothing more constructive. He steps aside at the first brush with the purposeful Octavius, and abdicates decision and final authority without protest. . . .

In an extraordinary speech rationalizing an impending assassination, Brutus acknowledges that Caesar is an impartial administrator of justice: "I have not known when his affections swayed / More than his reason." In order to kill friend, benefactor, and ruler, Brutus must wrap himself in a cause. A divinely appointed king is his own cause; he does what is necessary to safeguard himself because he knows that his office is necessary to the state; and, like Henry V, he has no qualms about executing traitors. But a rebel or assassin must act as the representative of something larger than himself, otherwise planned murder becomes impossible. . . .

It takes the ominous, heavily stressed lines of Antony's servant to bring Cassius and Brutus back to their real situation.

They do not get a chance to act out what they had planned, the role of liberators, which called for the highly theatrical waving of red weapons over their heads, and the crying out in the streets, "Peace, freedom, and liberty!" It is not surprising that Antony quickly takes command of what is going on, and it is soon evident that of all those who assume power, Brutus is the least equipped for action in the public world.

A ruler with a "public personality" is able to stand clear of his own confused, personal desires and plans, as well as those of others. Caesar could do this. Brutus could never cut free of his moral and aristocratic inheritance; Cassius of his hatred of Caesar and love of Brutus. . . .

Tyranny or Anarchy

In the absence of a natural leader who can control events strongly enough to make history, not merely endure it, every action offers a series of open options, an unending procession of ambiguous choices—and perhaps that is why *Julius Caesar* is above all a play of ambiguities and alternatives. The noblest Roman of them all fails miserably in everything but the form of his intent, and brings actual ruin and injustice by trying to forestall them. The triumvirs who arbitrarily select their relatives for death are a kind of nightmare projection of the tyranny Brutus feared might grow from Caesar's kingship. The vain, superstitious Caesar correctly feared Cassius and the omens; but, he did not act to forestall his fears. Flavius and Marullus were "put to silence" for insulting Caesar the ruler; no one—not even Casius—suffers because he seems a threat to Caesar the man.

Without an office that ensures justice, public life becomes the web of conflicting virtues and vices that we see after Caesar's death. At the end we are left with a military leader who is efficient but unsympathetic; indeed, Shakespeare's successful, impersonal rulers—Henry V, Octavius Caesar—appear as colorless men who, having integrated or eliminated conflicting emotions, are cold and calculating, more like impersonal institutions than individuals whose energy and appeal come from a conflict of allegiances. However, as *Julius Caesar* demonstrates, people of high ideals and good intentions are *too* emotional; ambition has never taught them the facts of public life, and they cannot make events obey them. The dilemma is simple but profound, and in our time is again reduced to its barest terms—anarchy or tyranny; and it plays itself out as it did in the Capitol [where Caesar was slain], but not on a stage, and with real blood.

Shakespeare Offers an Alternative to State-Mediated Social Order

Daniel Juan Gil

Daniel Juan Gil, a professor at Texas Christian University, is the author of Before Intimacy: Asocial Sexuality in Early Modern England.

In this viewpoint Gil describes Julius Caesar's *departure from the typical celebration of the state's intrusion into the lives of its citizens. Rather, claims Gil, William Shakespeare challenges "the nation-state as a basic framework for society." He introduces the battle between absolute rule and republicanism in the play but dismantles those ideologies by revealing the conflicting values and actions of the characters who champion those respective ideologies. When the mob prevails and Antony speaks after Caesar's death, Gil sees in the social disorganization an antipolitical rebellion. The inversion of social constructions undermines Rome's sociopolitical fabric and forces an alternative antipolitical ideology onto the bare scene.*

Many early modern writers, including [William] Shakespeare, celebrated the state's growing penetration of daily life. On the other hand, because the social imaginary founded on the nation-state was still emergent in the period, early modern writers, again including Shakespeare, could also conceive of alternatives. In that sense, the surviving literary culture of the period is a resource for rethinking some of our most basic modern assumptions about social and political life. My aim in these pages is to disclose an oppositional discourse that declines to assume the nation-state as a basic framework for society. . . .

The Impulse to Be Free of the State

The play [*Julius Caesar*] registers and theorizes the efforts of the state to reorganize social life, but the play also reveals a deep-seated impulse to break with this emerging political framework. While the conspirators in the play are often interpreted as defining a public sphere that resists Caesar's expansion of state power, the play rather points to a deep complicity between Caesar and the conspirators against him. By forcing social questions into a nationalized political frame of reference, their conflict consolidates and strengthens the national political field, which comes to attain almost a monopoly on the ways in which social life can be conceptualized. Marc Antony's rebellion must be understood against this backdrop. His is a rebellion not for Caesar or against Brutus (conceived as rival political positions) but against politics—against the acquiescence in a politics that orders social life into rival factions demanding personal sacrifice in the name of public goods. Antony teaches Rome a grammar of interpersonal bonding that defines connections between bodies (via emotions conceived as fluids), and these connections are meant to replace any politically mediated public life. Antony's oppositional discourse sounds irrational, unfeasible, or antisocial. But from a standpoint outside the political field (and that standpoint is what I am trying to locate), radical opposition is not antisocial so much as it is antisystemic—a clear break from the emerging, modern assumption of the nation-state as a fundamental condition of social life.

The political field that Shakespeare sketches in *Julius Caesar* is organized around the competing discursive poles of absolutism and elite civic republicanism. Caesar is accused of incipient tyranny, but within the terms of early modern political discourse his reliance on a blend of charismatic popularity and manipulation of aristocratic elites would make him look to Shakespeare's audience very much like an absolute monarch. To secure his grip on the political order, Caesar brings into being an abstract public of more or less formally interchangeable individuals who encounter the state as a spectacle that they either applaud or hoot. Caesar's absolutist program is counterbalanced by the civic republicanism of Brutus and the conspirators, for whom the state exists to offer an aristocratic elite opportunities for the exercise of virtue and thus the pursuit of ethical perfection. From the perspective of the conspirators, the state is constituted by patricians seeking to maximize their honor. Brutus and the conspirators deploy this conception of the state to delegitimize the popular public that Caesar has forced onto the political field. But more crucial than their differences is the similarity of these opponents: each party takes the rival version of political publicity into account, which attests to their differences being essentially local variations within a single political field. Caesar and the conspirators against him share a presupposition that political forms can create publics and structure a nationalized social life. It is this presumption that Antony will transcend.

The Conspirators' Identity Crisis

A familiar interpretation of *Julius Caesar* is that the conspirators represent a nascent public sphere that checks the dictatorial state power that Caesar represents. But the conspirators do not see themselves as operating outside the state or as speaking up for the presumed rights of some extra-state public; their main difficulty is that they cannot envision themselves and their exercise of virtue outside the framework of the state. Cassius experiences loss of political power as a diminution of self because for him the state is a vehicle to exercise and develop his own virtue. In his initial temptation speech,

Cassius reminds Brutus that "I was born free as Caesar, so were you" and complains that they have both become Caesar's "underlings":

Why, man, he doth bestride the narrow world

Like a colossus, and we petty men

Walk under his huge legs and peep about

To find ourselves dishonorable graves.

Men at some time are masters of their fates.

The fault, dear Brutus, is not in our stars,

But in ourselves, that we are underlings.

The fundamental problem is not that Caesar wants too much power but that he organizes state power on a footing that deprives aristocrats like Cassius and Brutus of their opportunity to use the state in service of their own honor. When Brutus invokes the discourse of the "general good," he refers only to the elite public of patricians that is constituted by, and constitutive of, the state.

In the civic republican tradition, individual rights are not an issue, though a small public of individual subjects is thought to underpin a state that enables them to pursue individual perfection. Thus, the conspirators in *Julius Caesar* regard plebeians as living an institutionalized, state-regulated life that, as a fundamentally economic formation, is the opposite of their own and improperly involved in public affairs. The play begins with Murellus and Flavius, the tribunes of the people and ideological soulmates of the conspirators, complaining that the workers are swarming into the streets to celebrate Caesar. Part of Murellus and Flavius's complaint is that the political allegiance of the people is fickle since they once loved Pompey as now they love Caesar [as Murellus comments to the commoners in the following]:

Many a time and oft

Have you climbed up to walls and battle-
ments,

To towers and windows, yea, to chimney
tops,

Your infants in your arms, and there have
sat

The livelong day with patient expectation

To see great Pompey pass the streets of
Rome.

But what Murellus and Flavius most object to is the
workers' leaving behind their defined roles in the economic
realm and asserting for themselves a role in the public life of
politics [as Flavius comments to the commoners in the fol-
lowing]:

Hence! home, you idle creatures, get you
home!

Is this a holiday? What, know you not,

(Being mechanical) you ought not to walk

Upon a labouring day without the sign

Of your profession? Speak, what trade art
thou?

The plebeians have left the nonpolitical but state-regulated
domain of the economy, where they wore the "sign / Of [their]
profession." Now unmarked, they appear to Murellus and Flavius as a shapeless mass that swarms over the architecture of
Rome carrying, as an index of vulgarity, their "infants in
[their] arms." Flavius promises to "drive away the vulgar from
the streets" and advises Murellus, "So do you too, where you
perceive them thick." . . .

In this still from the 1953 film production of William Shakespeare's Julius Caesar, *Mark Antony (played by Marlon Brando) speaks to the mob following Caesar's death.* The Kobal Collection.

The Antipolitical Rebellion

The amorphous crowd that appears in Rome at the margins of competing political visions exceeds all available political forms and yet it finds ways to assert itself more and more radically after Caesar is killed. Immediately following the assassination, Trebonius reports that "Men, wives, and children stare, cry out, and run, / As it were doomsday," and Brutus recognizes the danger: he asks Antony to "be patient till we have appeased / The multitude, beside themselves with fear." Brutus tells Cassius, "go you into the other street, / And part the numbers," while proposing to the plebeians that "Those that will hear me speak, let 'em stay here. / Those that will follow Cassius, go with him / And public reasons shall be rendered. Of Caesar's death." This image of an orderly exercise of public reasoning must warm the heart of Habermasians [pragmatists] committed to a universally human exercise of communicative rationality. But while one plebeian does suggest to the others that they listen to both speeches and then "compare their reasons / When severally we hear them rendered," Brutus's clumsy effort to address the mass as though it were a debating club only highlights his inability to come to terms with what the massed populace represents. A clash of rival versions of politically mediated social life has resulted in the displacement of society itself by a feral but now constitutive "bare life."

The brilliance of Marc Antony's funeral oration, in contrast to that of Brutus, derives largely from Antony's exploiting the experience of "bare life" as a source of antipolitical rage. But Antony's oration draws on his own experience of "bare life," undergone on the death of his friend: immediately after the assassination, Brutus tells Antony that he too loved Caesar but that this personal tie was necessarily secondary to public considerations. Antony, on the other hand, is drawn beyond political logic into rebellion against any notion of state-mediated social life. He refuses to regard the assassination as a political act or a political problem, and his irrational commitment to loving Caesar produces a crisis (or perhaps it is a breakthrough) in his experience of himself and others. Addressing Caesar's corpse, Antony promises that "a curse shall light upon the limbs of men," and he calls forth anarchic violence:

O pardon me, thou bleeding piece of earth,

That I am meek and gentle with these butchers.

Thou art the ruins of the noblest man

That ever lived in the tide of times.

Woe to the hand that shed this costly blood.

Over thy wounds now I do prophesy

(Which like dumb mouths do ope their
ruby lips

To beg the voice and utterance of my
tongue)

A curse shall light upon the limbs of men:

Domestic fury and fierce civil strife

Shall cumber all the parts of Italy:

Blood and destruction shall be so in use,

And dreadful objects so familiar,

That mothers shall but smile when they behold

Their infants quartered with the hands of
war:

All pity choked with custom of fell deeds,

And Caesar's spirit, ranging for revenge,

With Ate by his side come hot from hell,

Shall in these confines with a monarch's
voice

Cry havoc and let slip the dogs of war . . .

Dismantling Social Life Itself

Antony could have used the opportunity to define a political
program or to demand violence against evildoers—against all
who had opposed Caesar. Instead, his prophecy of violence
seems designed only to validate his own love for Caesar. It is
as if Antony feels that politics has split a nuclear bond between Caesar and himself, a bond whose violation must now
release an enormous burst of energy that will negate traditional social ties. Antony's cruel soliloquy has the merit of not
concealing beneath patriotic rhetoric the naked reality of frat-
ricide and war. But in precisely its cruelest aspects, his speech

also expresses a wish for transformation of the most basic patterns of society, including the structure of family allegiances. When Antony looks forward to a time in which mothers are so hardened to violence that they will "but smile when they behold / Their infants quartered," he is imagining a radical (if radically dystopian) change in social life that flows from his own disorienting experience of the body of Caesar. Antony seems drawn and captured by the unsettling gravity of a corpse whose "dumb mouths do ope their ruby lips / To beg the voice and utterance of my tongue." Here the opened body of Caesar summons Antony to enter and occupy it, to speak for it, to mingle with its fluids and especially its blood—a fantasy that had earlier led Antony to wish that he had "as many eyes as thou hast wounds, / Weeping as fast as they stream forth thy blood." ...

In this fantasy, bodies communicate by means of humoral fluids that produce pre- or extra-social links. ...

The funeral oration triggers rioting, and Antony celebrates the "it" he has unleashed: "Now let it work. Mischief, thou art afoot: / Take thou what course thou wilt." But however irrational, the rioting has a logic that picks up and extends the body-centered bonding that Antony experiences in relation to Caesar. Here is the beginning of the riot:

FIRST PLEBEIAN: Never, never. Come, away, away.

We'll burn his body in the holy place,

And with the brands fire the traitors' houses.

Take up the body.

SECOND PLEBEIAN: Go fetch fire.

THIRD PLEBEIAN: Pluck down benches.

FOURTH PLEBEIAN: Pluck down forms, windows, anything.

What begins as a recognizably political impulse—to cremate Caesar's body in the "holy place" and then set fire to the conspirators' houses—turns quickly into an eschatological desire to transcend politics as such. In attacking the benches and the windows (the benches on which they sat listening to competing accounts of the assassination; the windows through which people, not least Portia, glimpse public doings), these plebeians pull down the material infrastructure of the public life into which Caesar and the conspirators have equally drawn them. So seen, the masses' rage is an antipublic rage, a rage against publicity and politics.

Once liberated from any political framework, the riot, it is commonly argued, demonstrates to Shakespeare's audience the dangers of a people unconstrained by law and social order. But even the cruelest and most irrational elements of the rebellion—even the attack on Cinna the poet, mistaken initially for Cinna the conspirator—can be interpreted differently:

CINNA: I am Cinna the poet, I am Cinna the poet.

FOURTH PLEBEIAN: Tear him for his bad verses, tear him for his bad verses.

CINNA: I am not Cinna the conspirator.

FOURTH PLEBEIAN: It is no matter, his name's Cinna. Pluck but his name out of his heart, and turn him going.

THIRD PLEBEIAN: Tear him, tear him!

Violence and Self-Destruction

Though here, once again, the plebeians begin with a nominally political aim—to kill conspirators—by the time they have established that the Cinna at their mercy is not Cinna the conspirator, an undifferentiated frenzy for blood has taken over. On the one hand, there is a social logic to the frenzy, for in rebelling against Cinna's very name the plebeians are expressing resentment against those who have names as opposed to those who have none—the plebeians, after all, are assigned only numbers. On the other hand, the plebeians are not engaged in an act of compensatory status-building: they reduce themselves to the status of bodies (as agents of physical violence) while reducing Cinna to the same level (as an object of physical violence). "Pluck but his name out of his heart" is not an exclamation from a scene of ordinary mob violence. Names represent a basic principle of social differentiation, and this mob wants to reduce names to bodies. It is unclear whether Cinna survives this assault (the stage directions give us only "Exeunt all the Plebeians" [that is, the plebeians exit the stage]). But if he survives and walks (or is even dragged) off stage, it could look, from the vantage point of the theater audience, as though Cinna has been absorbed into the mob.

It is of course only as theater—the theater Antony loves— that violence can stand for a mode of sociability that operates at the level of bodies. When approached as a theatrical spectacle, the civil war that occupies the last two acts of the play seems an irrational outbreak of resistance to the politics of the nation-state—a political order to which Caesar and his assassins, as well as Queen Elizabeth and her antagonists, appear fully committed. Among the disturbing features of Shakespeare's civil war is the way that commonsensical, self-preserving forms of relationship are infected by the marginal experiences of self and other that Antony injects into Rome. The turn away from self-preservation is clear in the rash of suicides that overtakes the play, beginning with Portia's death after she has "swallowed fire"—said to be burning coals, in Plutarch [*Lives* by the ancient Greek and Roman historian Plutarch]—and continuing with the suicides of Cassius, Titinius, and finally Brutus. Given the Roman cult of suicide, these deaths could be read as triumphs of personal autonomy over fate. In Shakespeare's telling, however, the suicides are more problematic, for the public prestige of the Roman aristocrats who die is supplanted by perverse forms of bonding. When Cassius cannot find the courage to kill himself, he must beg his slave Pindarus for death:

Come hither, sirrah.

In Parthia did I take thee prisoner,

And then I swore thee, saving of thy life,

That whatsoever I did bid thee do,

Thou shouldst attempt it. Come now, keep
thine oath.

Now be a freeman, and with this good
sword

That ran through Caesar's bowels, search
this bosom.

Cassius consciously frames the circumstances of his own death as poetic justice: his dying words are, "Caesar, thou art revenged, / Even with the sword that killed thee." But the fantasy of being penetrated by the sword that "ran through Caesar's bowels"—the same fantasy that possessed Antony after the assassination—is a way of reestablishing a relationship with Caesar at a level well below that of political allegiance and class solidarity (or even homosociality: the object of the fantasy is a corpse that Cassius helped to mutilate).

Social Inversion

This perverse form of bonding, moreover, depends on the inversion of a functionally hierarchical tie between master and slave. "Go show your slaves how choleric you are," Brutus taunts Cassius for losing his temper, "And make your bondmen tremble." It is to his bondman that Cassius, a Roman lord begging ardently for death, finally turns himself over—and the spectacle is repeated with Brutus begging for death at the hands of his servant Strato. In both instances, the relationship between master and slave turns out to be the only reliable one. But Shakespeare takes this bond out of its social context, where it has large consequences for both master and slave, and relocates it in a purely emotional space. The mediated aggression of massive class disparity then fuels a lurid exchange between men that combines aggressive passion with passionate aggression. For Cassius, this suicidal inversion is triggered by what turns out to be an incorrect report of the death of Cassius's "best friend" Titinius: "O, coward that I am, to live so long, / To see my best friend ta'en before my face." Having failed to defend his friend in the moment when he is "ta'en," Cassius apparently regards suicide as a way of restoring their friendship. That renewal takes the form of a connection in which the fate of Titinius is registered in Cassius's own body. When Titinius, alive, returns to find that Cassius has "misconstrued everything," he promptly stabs himself with the sword that killed Cassius: "By your leave, gods. This is a Roman's part: / Come, Cassius' sword, and find Titinius' heart." While Titinius comes closest in this string of suicides to the aristocratic ideal of dying with honor ("this is a Roman's part"), he nevertheless joins Cassius and Antony in affirming a corporeal solidarity that transcends social status: he uses the sword still gory with Cassius's blood (and Caesar's).

The male-male friendship of aristocrats and the asymmetrical bond between master and slave—but also the stoical mastery over self that Cassius and Brutus so spectacularly lack—are social ties and functions upon which real-world status depends. Shakespeare has character after character in *Julius Caesar* reject social expectations and open an alternative way of being, in which bleeding bodies are penetrated by already bloody swords. It is important to read such moments, and indeed the civil war as a whole, for what they open the door to philosophically; or rather, theatrically. Ignited and then pervaded by antisocial and fundamentally perverse desires, the play's civil war is not a continuation of politics by other means but a frantic escape from and replacement for politics. Bringing this war to the early modern stage, Shakespeare offered an alternative to the iron clasp of the state and of state-mediated social order. The seeming inhumanity of the alternative is a measure of how deeply felt the revulsion from that social order could be. Read against the grain of the modern political imaginary, which assumes the nation-state as the basic framework for social life, and social life as a necessity of human beings, this play discloses a passionate dissent of bodies from the political and social penetration of "bare life."

Julius Caesar Challenges the Renaissance Debate over Tyrannicide

Robert S. Miola

Robert S. Miola is the Gerard Manley Hopkins Professor of English at Loyola University. He is the author of Shakespeare's Rome.

In this viewpoint Miola explores the question of what qualities a tyrant possesses and whether the murder of any tyrant is justified—problems that were debated often and vigorously in William Shakespeare's day. Opposing views of Caesar went to extremes, some arguing that he was the benign ruler of the Roman world and others justifying his assassination. In Miola's view Shakespeare denies aspects of Caesar's historical character and that of the opposition by applying political theory to their motives and actions. For example, Miola reveals how Caesar of the play is a tyrant according to his methods of achieving power and using power. But, Miola contends, Shakespeare also justifies Caesar's power by revealing the opposition's questionable motives and highlighting Caesar's warm and trusting attitude to the opposition itself. By discovering tyrannical qualities in those determined to bring the tyrant down and republican virtues in the tyrant, the play challenges easy judgments, Miola concludes.

Elizabethan plays, especially [William] Shakespeare's histories and tragedies, reflect the political turmoil and the current absorption with tyrannicide.

A significant point of dispute in the tyrannicide debate was the controversial assassination of Julius Caesar. Unlike

Robert S. Miola, "*Julius Caesar* and the Tyrannicide Debate," *Renaissance Quarterly*, Summer 1985, pp. 272–78, 280–83, 288–89. Published by University of Chicago Press. Copyright © 1985 by Renaissance Quarterly. Reproduced by permission of the publisher and author.

Nero, Domitian, and Caligula—all universally reviled as hateful tyrants—Caesar evoked the full spectrum of Renaissance opinion and so did his assassination. [Italian humanist Coluccio] Salutati, for example, praised Caesar as "the father of his country, the lawful and benignant ruler of the world" and justified [Italian poet of the Middle Ages] Dante's consignment of the traitors Brutus and Cassius to the lowest circle of hell. [Spanish philosopher Francisco] Suarez, however, condemned Caesar as a usurper of sovereign power "through violence and tyranny," lauded the assassination, and seconded [Roman philosopher] Cicero's praise of Brutus and Cassius's courage. The medieval John of Salisbury and the late Renaissance John Milton, like many others, took a position between the extremes: both recognized that Caesar unlawfully assumed power and in so doing acted the part of a tyrant; but both also expressed regret about the assassination, respecting Caesar's virtues and showing ambivalence toward Brutus and Cassius. Still others, like [English historian] Richard Reynoldes and [English playwright and historian] William Fulbecke, took no serious and consistent stand, contenting themselves instead with solemn moralizations as well as various and contradictory political bromides about the evils of pride, tyranny, *and* rebellion.

The tyrannicide debate, featuring Caesar in a prominent and polemical position, contributes much to the form and substance of Shakespeare's *Julius Caesar*. This debate defined precisely those questions important to the play: how to tell a tyrant from a just king; how to tell envious murderers from heroic republicans; how and when to justify assassination. The tyrannicide debate aired all the major issues of the play and set forth the criteria for judgment likely to be used by contemporary audiences. . . .

The Meaning of the Word in the Play

The word "tyrant" and its cognates are crucially important to the play. The plebeian [general Roman citizens'] identification of Caesar as tyrant echoes other references. Cassius avers that suicide can defeat "tyrants" and "tyranny"; he queries: "And why should Caesar be a tyrant then?" Brutus incites the others against "high-sighted tyranny." After the assassination the conspirators proclaim, "Liberty! Freedom! Tyranny is dead!" At the end of the play Young Cato pronounces himself "A foe to tyrants." Yet the plebeians who confidently pronounce Caesar a tyrant soon mourn the fallen leader and seek revenge on the traitors who slew him. The term "tyrant" in this play . . . evokes an important set of criteria for judging the assassination.

Examination of the term "tyrant" can clarify the nature of these criteria. In antiquity the term referred to a ruler who came to power by usurpation, without constitutional warrant. In the works of Plato, Aristotle [both classical Greek philosophers], and others, however, the term came to describe any evil ruler, any one who governed by whim for personal gain instead of by law for the general welfare. Deriving mainly from Aristotle, long lists like the exhaustive catalogue of Egidius Romanus Colonna itemized the distinctive characteristics of tyrants and kings and contrasted their styles of government. Medieval and Renaissance theorists, notably Aquinas and Bartolus, officially recognized both the earlier and later conceptions of tyrants, declaring that a man could prove himself a tyrant in entrance, *ex defectu tituli*, or in execution *ex parte exercitil*. By Shakespeare's day, then, the term "tyrant" could apply to any usurper of power by force as well as to any lawful ruler who governed viciously.

Caesar's Entrance to Power

Does Shakespeare depict Caesar as a tyrant "in entrance," *ex defectu tituli*? Cassius repeatedly emphasizes the unnaturalness of Caesar's rise to power. According to him, Caesar is a feeble mortal who has, incredibly, now "become a god." Cassius queries: "Upon what meat doth this our Caesar feed / That he is grown so great?" Images of hideously unnatural growth, op-

An often debated topic in Shakespeare's day was represented with the murder scene of Julius Caesar *in the Shakespearean play of the same name: Whether the murder of a tyrant is justified.* © Donald Cooper/Photostage. Reproduced by permission.

posed to the normal processes of maturation and development, appear again in the storm scene. The monstrous portents of the strange night, according to Cassius, reflect the disorder of "A man no mightier than thyself, or me, / In personal action, yet prodigious grown." After pointing to Caesar's human frailty—his near-drowning in the Tiber [River], his fever in Spain—Cassius compares him to a "Colossus," a huge, artificial, and empty construction. Cassius here echoes several contemporary tyrannicide discussions, wherein the Colossus simile likewise describes the tyrant about to fall. . . .

In the play Murellus and Flavius rebuke the populace for celebrating Caesar's victory over "Pompey's blood." Not merely guilty of impropriety, these commoners are guilty of hypocrisy, self-interest, and ingratitude. The reference to "Pompey's blood," i.e., to his sons, also suggests the sin of *impietas* [impiety]. These Romans applaud the conqueror whose sword carves up Roman families and cuts the line of future Roman citizens.

The references to Roman history also suggest the unconstitutionality of Caesar's entrance to power. The story of Junius Brutus's revolt against the tyrannical Tarquin, twice alluded to in the play, reminds the audience, as it does the later Brutus, that Roman government was representative. Government by a single ruler violated Roman constitutional and legal traditions and signalled the degeneration of the city and its inhabitants. . . .

Clearly, evidence in the play indicates that Shakespeare's Caesar, then, is a tyrant *ex defectu tituli*. From this perspective Brutus' resolve to think Caesar "as a serpent's egg, / Which, hatch'd, would as his kind, grow mischievous" and to "kill him in the shell" is perfectly proper and expedient. For the tyrant in entrance, a significant number agreed, had to be slain as soon as possible, before his tyranny could gain rooting or, worse yet, legitimacy through oath or pact. . . .

Shakespeare Justifies Caesar's Leadership

Shakespeare, however, does not let the case rest so easily; he takes care to justify Caesar's entrance to power. Cassius, the man who paints a picture of Caesar as a tyrant, is lean and hungry, a character with questionable motives and methods. Adroitly he flatters Brutus and appeals to his ambition.

> Brutus and Caesar: what should be in that
> "Caesar"?
>
> Why should that name be sounded more
> than yours?

In a soliloquy early in the play, he makes a sinister observation: "Well, Brutus, thou art noble; yet I see / Thy honourable mettle may be wrought / From that it is dispos'd." He rejoices at the success of his plot in language that suggests corruption and deceit: "For who so firm that cannot be seduc'd?" In order to enlist Brutus in the conspiracy he resorts to forgery:

I will this night,

In several hands, in at his windows throw,

As if they came from several citizens,

Writings, all tending to the great opinion

That Rome holds of his name; wherein ob-
scurely

Caesar's ambition shall be glanced at.

Shakespeare radically changes Plutarch here, who records in the "Life of Caesar" and in the "Life of Brutus" that the people wrote letters to Brutus and cast them upon his chair. The changing of the popular appeal into a cheap trick darkens the character of Cassius and makes suspect his motivations and judgment.

The impression that the conqueror of "Pompey's blood" is, *ipso facto* [by that fact], a tyrant in entrance is also counterbalanced and qualified. Again Shakespeare alters received tradition to legitimize Caesar's rise to power. Most historians and commentators agreed that Antony's offering of the crown and Caesar's subsequent refusals were parts of a political charade, a test of the people by the ambitious would-be ruler. Shakespeare, however, leaves the entire matter in some question. . . .

Caesar Acts Like a Tyrant

Shakespeare's Caesar has some of the salient characteristics of the tyrant in practice. He fears plots and conspiracies, twice observing early in the play that such men as Cassius are "dangerous." Despite stirring denunciations of fear, Caesar orders a sacrifice in response to the unnatural portents of the storm. Calphurnia persuades him of the threat to himself and he fashions an excuse for staying home, "Mark Antony shall say I am not well." He [Caesar] shows *superbia* arrogant pride, another distinguishing characteristic of the tyrant. Shakespeare's

Caesar considers himself a special creation, far superior to ordinary mortals. Cimber's supplication, Caesar avers. "Might fire the blood of ordinary men," but not his. Others are "flesh and blood, and apprehensive," but only Caesar "unassailable holds on his rank, / Unshak'd of motion." Such *superbia* leads Caesar to willfullness, another identifying mark of the tyrant. Citing Erasmus's discussion of tyrannical will, [literacy critic] Bernard R. Breyer observes that Caesar continually talks of his will in Act II Scene ii. After changing his mind and resolving not to go to the Senate, Caesar responds to Decius's request for a reason: "The cause is in my will, I will not come: / That is enough to satisfy the Senate." Such nonchalant substitution of personal caprice for just cause and law marks the tyrant in execution. That Caesar changes his mind once again and decides finally to go to the Senate underscores the arbitrariness of his will and, by extension, the instability of his tyrannical rule.

Shakespeare's Caesar not only looks and sounds like a tyrant, he acts like one. From Plutarch's brief and bland account of the petitions preceding the assassination, Shakespeare creates a highly charged scene of tyrannical action. First, Caesar announces that he and "his Senate" are ready to redress grievances, thus assuming ownership of the Roman legislative and judicial body. Then he imperiously refuses to repeal the decree banishing Cimber's brother: "If thou dost bend, and pray, and fawn for him, / I spurn thee like a cur out of my way." Caesar does not discuss the crime committed or the merits of the petition, but simply refers to his past decision, in other words, to his will. As Caesar was justly famous for his clemency and since, as Seneca and others declared, clemency was a characteristic virtue of a good king, Shakespeare takes pains here to mark Caesar's rule as tyrannical.

The self-love so flagrantly evident in Caesar's disregard for senatorial authority and for kingly virtue appears earlier in more subtle and more dangerous form. Caesar, we are told, puts the tribunes Murellus and Flavius "to silence" for pulling scarves off his images. Shakespeare changes Plutarch's "diadems" [crowns] to scarves to stress the triviality of the offense and thus to underline the severity of the punishment. Whereas Plutarch tells us that Caesar deprived the tribunes of their office, Shakespeare leaves their fate ominously uncertain, hinting at the possibility of murder. These alterations portray Caesar as vain, ruthless, and unjust, as a tyrant who capriciously punishes citizens who displease him. No wonder the stock animal metaphors for the tyrant cluster around Caesar. Cassius describes him as a wolf who preys on sheep, a lion on hinds. Brutus, we have noted, sees him as a serpent and later draws an image from falconry "So let high-sighted tyranny range on, / Till each man drop by lottery." For such a ruler, classical, medieval, and Renaissance authorities insisted, there could be only one end: a sudden and violent death. The assassination of Caesar in Act III, then, testifies strongly, if circumstantially, to his tyrannical character.

Caesar as Likable

Although Shakespeare endows Caesar with some of the attributes of a tyrant, he draws the portrait in light and shade, with many qualifying brushstrokes. Caesar may fear plots but he loves and trusts his fellow Romans. He is close to Antony and warmly invites Brutus and the other conspirators to share wine: "Good friends, go in, and taste some wine with me, / And we, like friends, will straightway go together." How unlike the typical tyrant who lives sequestered from his people, surrounded by a guard of foreign mercenaries. Kindly, he leaves to the people his "private arbors and new-planted orchards, / On this side Tiber," thus making all citizens "heirs for ever." ... After Artemidorus urges him to read a letter exposing the conspiracy, Caesar responds, "What touches us ourself shall be last serv'd," and sweeps on to his death. Shakespeare here diverges from Plutarch's account, wherein Caesar tries many times to read the letter but cannot because of the crowd; he portrays instead the self-sacrificing ruler more concerned with public welfare than his own.

It is true that Caesar is willful but so are others in the play. Brutus overrules the wishes of his fellows on at least three important decisions: 1) he urges the sparing of Antony; 2) he allows Antony to speak at Caesar's funeral; 3) he meets the enemy at Philippi. In fact, as some have noted, Brutus resembles Caesar in significant ways: both command the respect of Romans, both have night scenes with their wives, both proclaim their honor and Romanitas, both spurn fear of death. In quarrel with Cassius, Brutus sounds the note of self-glorification prominent in Caesar's northern star speech:

There is no terror, Cassius, in your threats;

For I am arm'd so strong in honesty

That they pass by me as the idle wind,

Which I respect not.

This series of parallels may ironically reveal tyrannical tendencies in the self-proclaimed tyrant-slayer. . . .

A Play of Ambivalence

In *Julius Caesar* no trustworthy source of sovereignty arises to direct Rome; there is only the politics of the marketplace, a confusing cacophony of claims and counterclaims. In this world the origins of civil government and sovereignty lie in the possession of power, pure, simple, and amoral.

The treatises on tyrannicide shape *Julius Caesar* in important ways: they define its political and moral framework and structure its ambivalences. From the tyrannicide debate Shakespeare creates a work which challenges its origins, those confident, fiercely advocative polemics on politics and morals. For the play dramatizes the differences between history, mysterious and unpredictable, and political theory; life resists legal definition and the formulations of jurists. *Julius Caesar* reveals only too clearly the difficulty of judging rulers, of categorizing them as tyrants or kings. It exposes also the difficulties inherent in tyrannicide—the temptation of self-interest, the lurking corruptions of deceit and political demagoguery, the ever-threatening danger of the untrammeled consequence.

Shakespeare Presents All Characters Sympathetically

Francis Fergusson

Francis Fergusson was professor of English literature at Rutgers University. He is the author of several books, including The Idea of a Theater.

In this selection Fergusson considers Julius Caesar's *classification as a tragedy and the touching fellowships and rivalries that have likely inspired the play's popularity since its creation. In the midst of widely differing views of the play's heroic and tragic characters, Fergusson argues that the play contains no single hero but treats all characters sympathetically. Caesar demonstrates heroic and tragic qualities, but his significance in the context of the play is defined in relation to the surrounding characters. William Shakespeare reveals in Brutus and Antony both strengths and weaknesses, grounded in domestic scenes and emotional motivations, claims Fergusson. And the end of the play, Fergusson asserts, is touching and ironic as the characters recognize their own failings and the others' integrity.*

Julius *Caesar* was written in 1599, about a year before *Hamlet*. It is usually called the first of [William] Shakespeare's tragedies, and "tragic" it certainly is, for it begins with the murder of Caesar and ends with the suicides of Brutus and Cassius. But in this play Shakespeare was not exploring the frontiers of human experience, and it does not have the terror and mystery we feel in *Hamlet*. The scene is warm and human; the story is that of the rivalries of vigorous men who know and love each other like brothers. It is exciting, bloody, and very touching, but even in its catastrophe it is full of the joy of life and battle. Perhaps that is why it has been popular ever since Shakespeare first produced it with his own fellow-actors.

Shakespeare had written *Titus Andronicus* at the beginning of his career, and plays on Roman themes were popular well before his *Julius Caesar*. There were no doubt plays about Caesar himself (now lost), for old Polonius had acted in one when he was at the university: "I did enact Julius Caesar," he tells Hamlet; "I was killed i' th' Capitol; Brutus killed me." But the only certain source of the play is [ancient Greek and Roman historian] Plutarch's *Lives*, in [Thomas] North's translation. Shakespeare is faithful to the facts which Plutarch presents in his *Caesar, Brutus,* and *Antony* [chapters], and in several details he is close to North's actual language. But the theme and structure of the play are his own. He concentrates Plutarch's three rather leisurely narratives into one of the fastest and most exciting of his plays.

He starts the story at the end of Caesar's career, as that conqueror is returning in triumph to Rome, very shortly before the murder. At that moment in Roman history the virtuous old Roman Republic was in decline. Its august Senate, the guardian of law, had been bullied for years by a succession of victorious generals, who were bidding against each other for supreme power in the state. Caesar and Pompey were such generals. Shakespeare (who had read his history) knew that the Republic was doomed, and that Octavius Caesar would soon establish the Empire. But some of the "noblest Romans," like Brutus and Cassius, were still loyal to the Republic and its ancient freedom under law; they were prepared to die rather than accept a monarchy. The common people, meanwhile, had lost faith in the Senators and the Tribunes, and they were ready for a strong man—Caesar or Pompey—who would promise to safeguard their interests. Shakespeare presents this situation in a few bold strokes in the first two scenes of Act I. The Roman crowd is veering from Pompey to Caesar; Caesar himself has the natural authority, the magic touch, of the born ruler. But the Tribunes in scene 1 and Brutus and Cassius in scene 2 share none of the popular enthusiasm for Caesar. They see in him a deadly threat to their own rights and privileges as citizens of the old Republic. By the end of scene 2 the action of the play is already in motion: a many-sided struggle to control Rome. Will the old Republican liberties be restored, or will Rome yield to the all-powerful spirit of Caesar and become a monarchy?

Why Caesar's Spirit Triumphs

There is no difficulty whatever in following this struggle as Shakespeare presents it. Against a background of popular discontent, fear, and superstition, with sinister omens of trouble to come, Cassius and Brutus form their conspiracy, while Caesar tries to play his new role as head of state. The climax and turning point come (as usual in Shakespeare's plays) in the middle of Act III. Brutus and Cassius succeed, at that point, in murdering Caesar; but that is their last success. Antony in his famous funeral oration turns the crowd against the conspirators, and civil war follows at once between Antony and Octavius Caesar on one side and Brutus and Cassius on the other. Acts IV and V present that savage war, ending in Brutus' and Cassius' defeat at Philippi; and also the quarrels which develop between Antony and Octavius, and between Brutus and Cassius. In this chaos, where every man is against every other man, "Caesar's spirit" triumphs even in death.

Differing Views of Shakespeare and Brutus

Though the story of the play is clear and unmistakable, its meaning has been interpreted in various ways by readers who want to make one of the fighting Romans the "hero." In our time Brutus is the favorite, because of his republican principles. Thus some years ago, when [Benito] Mussolini and [Adolf] Hitler were newly in power, Mr. Orson Welles made a very stimulating modern-dress [theater] production, in which Caesar was presented as a modern type of dictator, and Brutus as an embattled democrat or liberal. Shakespeare sees Brutus so sympathetically that he does make a good hero; but (as Mr. Welles's version showed) one cannot interpret the whole play that way without making drastic cuts, especially in Acts IV and V. There is really no "hero"; all the characters are sympathetically presented; and if one wants to grasp the play as Shakespeare wrote it one must learn to see the delicate "balance" he keeps between the main characters. The play is balanced upon the significant and mysterious figure of Caesar: all of the political issues, and the motives of all the characters, depend on Caesar the man and Caesar the symbol of Empire. What are we to make of him?

He is presented very briefly. His first appearance as he makes his way through the adoring crowd—controlled, shrewd, and detached—is impressive. But when we see him at home trying to decide whether to go to the Capitol in spite of the ill omens, he is indecisive. He is, however, not so much frightened as puzzled: he wants to find out what fate, or the gods, want him to do. In the Capitol when the conspirators try to make him revoke his banishment of Publius Cimber, he sounds pompous:

I could be well moved, if I were as you;

If I could pray to move, prayers would move me.

But I am constant as the northern star,

Of whose true-fixed and resting quality

There is no fellow in the firmament.

We must remember that Shakespeare always sees his tragic characters with irony. When he gets ready to "carve them as a dish fit for the gods" he shows the pride or blindness which dooms them, as well as their greatness. Moreover, Caesar himself is consciously playing the role of supreme authority in Rome, trying to act, as well as *be*, the incorruptible ruler which the confusion of the times demands. The people recognize that authority in him, but there is no precedent for it in Rome; and Caesar finds the role rather new and strange.

The character of Caesar is interesting, but his significance is brought out by the other characters who love or hate him. Everyone in the play is deeply committed to the passionate game of politics, with Caesar in the center. As the game swirls around him the other characters show his meaning from their various points of view, and at the same time they reveal themselves completely in their relationships to him.

Views of the Conspirators

Cassius shows his motives at once. According to Caesar Cassius "thinks too much," and it is true that he is always brooding and contriving. But he does not think like a philosopher, to discover the truth, but passionately, to win the game. In the Roman free-for-all he cannot see why Caesar, whom he has known since school-days, should come out on top. . . .

Brutus has to think of the murder—and make the public think of it—as a just, even religious sacrifice. But in the staging of the murder, butchery is stressed; and when Antony comes he mocks the pretense of ceremony, and compares Caesar to a deer slaughtered by many hunters. The spirit of Caesar turns out to be stronger after the murder than before it. Brutus has little psychological insight; he is out of his depth in the situation which Cassius, and the course of Roman history, have forced upon him. But he is a strong, decent, simple man, and we know that he will take all the consequences of his decision without flinching.

It was a stroke of genius on Shakespeare's part to show us Brutus, on the night of his crucial decision, in his own household. In that setting he reminds one of the country-gentleman statesmen of our own early republic—[Thomas] Jefferson, say, or his friend [John] Adams. Brutus' boy, Lucius, with whom he has such a gentle human relationship, is there to serve him. His wife Portia, awakened by the nocturnal comings and go-ings, fears that Brutus is lost to her; but, though she is "as dear to me as are the ruddy drops / That visit my sad heart," Brutus cannot reassure her. The decision which separates him from Caesar also separates him from Portia and the love and loyalty which had joined them. This theme returns near the end of the play when Brutus tells Cassius, after their quarrel, that Portia has committed suicide, and then, while the faithful Lucius sleeps, sees Caesar's ghost.

Antony is as clearly defined as Brutus and Cassius. While Caesar lives he serves him naturally and without envy, enjoy-ing himself the while with military adventures and lots of late parties. But the moment Caesar is murdered he sees that henceforth, in Rome, it will be every man for himself; and he proceeds to play that dangerous game in a style of his own. He has no principles to make him stiff and awkward, like Brutus; he does not burn with envy of other men, like Cas-sius; and so he proves more free and resourceful than either of them. He keeps his own counsel and improvises brilliantly. He takes advantage of Brutus' integrity to speak at the funeral, and then, subtly feeling his way with the moods of the crowd, rouses them suddenly against the conspirators. When the war starts he is ruthless: with the cold-blooded Octavius he slaugh-ters every potential enemy he can lay hands on. He is a tough fighter, but full of warmth and charm, and when he gives his touching tribute to the dead Brutus at the end of the play we feel that his emotion is honest and generous. . . .

The fighting Romans are in a sense still loyal in feeling to Caesar; they are trying desperately to fill his place, but none of them can do it. In their failure and in the wider chaos of the war Caesar triumphs, as Brutus and Cassius both see after Philippi. By the end of the play all four leaders are somewhat tarnished, both physically and spiritually, by their violent battles; but when the pressure of fighting is removed, they recognize their errors and failures, as well as each other's gallantry. There is plenty of irony in the ending of the play, but no bitterness; and because the chief characters are so wonderfully and deeply human, their catastrophe is very touching.

Brutus's Noble Heroism
Is Superficial

James C. Bulman

An English professor at Allegheny College, James C. Bulman is the author of Comedy from Shakespeare to Sheridan.

According to Bulman in the viewpoint that follows, Caesar's heroism is ironic; he uses language to promote himself as a god, but physical and mental failings reveal his inability to rule. Nor is Brutus, the insurgent against tyranny, the "heroic justifier", that we might be led to believe, claims Bulman. Even though he thinks he has evidence of Caesar's greed for power, Brutus's fight for the people is only an outward pretense, and he advises his co-conspirators to put on an act to influence the populace. Bulman states that eventually Brutus comes to feel that he has joined the rebellion out of revenge, and when Brutus and Cassius speculate that their deeds will be later glorified and dramatized, the ironic theatricality of their plot is confirmed.

The idioms [William] Shakespeare employed to delineate heroism in his early plays were too restrictive to allow him a personal signature. It is not by chance that these plays for years were thought to be the work, or at least to contain the work, of other dramatists: they fully partake of the conventions that were the stock-in-trade of stage heroism. But together they constitute only Shakespeare's apprenticeship to already-established writers. Within a few years, he was forging a mimesis more sophisticated than any that had yet been tried and, as a consequence, was recutting the heroic patterns that only yesterday he had found fashionable enough. His new heroes were characterized by their awareness of conventional expectations, and their tragedies arose from their failure to live up to them—from their inability to wear hand-me-down roles with any comfort or conviction. The authenticity of the plays themselves sprang likewise from their simultaneous employment and repudiation of the conventions that had bodied forth a heroic reality in the "old plays."

The death of Caesar illustrates how Shakespeare had come to use conventions with detachment, even irony. *Julius Caesar* is often labeled a sort of revenge play, harking back to various Senecan plays on the theme of Caesar's hubris and perhaps directly to an academic play called *Caesar's Revenge.* . . .

With the hyperbole that has characterized all conqueror heroes, Caesar ingenuously identifies in himself an absolute integrity of self and self-image. . . . He is what he says he is—a godlike hero of mythic proportions. The language defines him as such; and public acclaim, heard offstage each time he refuses the crown, affirms it. But Shakespeare does not let this assertion stand unchallenged. Against that offstage acclaim, he gives us an antiphonal voice *on* stage that relentlessly, right up to the time of the murder, points out Caesar's naked frailties: he is deaf in one ear; he has epilepsy; Cassius once had to save him from drowning. Even his wife Calpurnia qualifies our admiration by gently mocking his vaunt as unwise boasting: "Alas, my lord, / Your wisdom is consum'd in confidence." In the judgment of various Renaissance historians, such hubris provided ample justification for Caesar's murder; and so Brutus characterizes it: "People and senators, be not affrighted. / Fly not; stand still. *Ambition's debt is paid.*"

Brutus's Weak Motives

But much as Brutus would like to conceive of Caesar's death as a moral exemplum, a just retribution in the tradition of the *Fall of Princes* [a series of tragedies by John Lydgate], he cannot: he is too circumspect to believe in the public construction he puts on it. Like a chivalric defender of national honor

In this illustration, Brutus is haunted by the ghost of Julius Caesar—a tyrant he helped murder. © Lebrect Music and Arts Photo Library/Alamy.

in the early histories, or even more like Titus who takes great risks to preserve Rome's honor, Brutus would define his role in Caesar's death as that of heroic justicer. He would prefer to regard the murder as consonant with public rather than private honor—

If it be aught toward the general good,

Set honor in one eye and death i' th' other,

And I will look on both indifferently;

—but he senses more deeply that his role likens him to a revenger who calls wrongs to a private accounting without recourse to law.

Brutus is aware that he has insufficient evidence of those "wrongs" to justify the murder. "To speak truth of Caesar, / I have not known when his affections sway'd / More than his reason." Thus, in order to persuade himself, he must conjecture some future cause and proceed to act on that conjecture as if it were proof:

And, since the quarrel

Will bear no color for the thing he is,

Fashion it thus. . . .

The vocabulary of his internal debate, "Fashion it thus," reveals in him an active will to dissemble. He will seek no "cavern" to mask the "monstrous visage" of conspiracy, but rather will "hide it in smiles and affability." Beyond the mask of smiles, he advocates a grander imposture that would disguise blood revenge in the cloak of ceremony. "Let's be sacrificers, but not butchers," he urges his fellow conspiracy:

And let our hearts, as subtle masters do,

Stir up their servants to an act of rage,

And after seem to chide 'em. This shall make

Our purpose necessary, and not envious;

Which so appearing to the common eyes,

We shall be call'd purgers, not murderers.

Brutus's Hypocrisy

Brutus's advice to his coconspirators is remarkably like Volumnia's to Coriolanus [in Shakespeare's Roman play *Coriolanus*]: as the public eye alone will determine the legitimacy of your heroic fame, act the part nobly, even if you do not believe in it. The pretense to heroism, reflected in the "seem" and the "so appearing," is ironic because Brutus would include his own among the "common eyes" he is trying to deceive. With a duplicity of which the more conventionally drawn heroes of Shakespeare's earlier plays were incapable, Brutus teaches his fellows to play a role to convince the audience of their integrity, and at the same time he would convince himself that the role is perfectly consistent with his ethical selfhood. He would be as absolute as Caesar in believing himself a hero. The traditional heroic vocabulary he uses conveys that wish: "our hearts," seats of the will, must stir "their servants," the passions, to "an act of rage," an essential component of heroes from Achilles onward. And why? Because murder resulting from a noble wrath will always be condoned as a heroic deed. So strong is Brutus's wish, in fact, that it almost fathers self-delusion.

His wish is undermined by the self-consciousness with which he uses the heroic idiom, however. In his attempt to use the idiom to effect only an *appearance* of heroic purpose, its credibility as a means of representing reality suffers. Brutus tries hard to convince us otherwise. To reinforce the legitimacy of his purpose, he resorts to a form of traditional oath-taking; but he metamorphoses it into a fellowship of honesty, suggesting that the reality of the oath transcends mere words: "What need we any spur but our own cause . . . And what other oath / Than honesty to honesty engag'd . . .?" Brutus adopts the ritual—"Give me your hands all over, one by one"—only to try to outdo it in high-minded pretense: "No, not an oath. If not the face of men, / The sufferance of our souls, the time's abuse—." But in declining the oath itself, in reaching instead for something more universal, he fails to engage himself with the form and with the power of its accumulated meaning that generations of heroes had counted on for sustenance. The self-consciousness with which he manipulates the form betrays his detachment from the ethos it signifies.

The Tyrant's Murder as a Theatrical Event

Brutus's failure to be engaged with the forms he enacts is dramatized even more explicitly in the murder of Caesar. Ritual murder scenes were a popular part of the revenge tradition. Shakespeare had played them to the hilt in his *Henry VI* plays, especially when Edward, Richard, and Clarence one by one stab young Prince Edward before his mother's eyes and again, even more sensationally, in the Thyestian banquet of blood that concludes the festivities in *Titus Andronicus.* Caesar himself had been ritually murdered in the academic *Caesar's Revenge,* falling to the music of Cassius's couplet, "Stab on, stab on, thus should your Poniards play, / Aloud deepe note upon this trembling Kay," and confronted at the last by Brutus's stern rebuke:

> But lives hee still, yet doth the Tyrant breath?
>
> Chalinging Heavens with his blasphemies,
>
> . . . .
>
> I bloody *Caesar, Caesar, Brutus* too,
>
> Doth greeve thee this, and this to quite *Romes* wrongs.

Shakespeare's Brutus, unlike his earlier counterpart, is not content simply to do the deed out of moral conviction. Rather, he arranges Caesar's murder as a theatrical event. He directs his accomplices to play their parts "as our Roman actors do, / With untir'd spirits and formal constancy"—an admission that constancy is no more to him than outward form—and bestows legitimacy on the murder by bidding them to bathe their hands in Caesar's blood, besmear their swords, then walk with him to the market-place,

> And, waving our red weapons o'er our heads,

> Let's all cry, "Peace, freedom, and liberty!"

Through these conventional signs of ritual sacrifice, Brutus hopes to persuade his audience of Romans that Caesar's murder was a heroic act—a purge of tyranny, as in the old play—and that he and his accomplices are liberators, Rome's saviors, not butchers. He and Cassius even speculate that players in "ages hence" will reenact this "lofty scene" to the glory of their memory. "How many times shall Caesar bleed in sport," Brutus ponders; and in so pondering, he "places" the event in a theatrical context and attempts to convince us, as well as himself, that outward shows may *create* a substantial reality.

Julius Caesar Was Staged Both to Promote and to Oppose Fascist Regimes

Michael Anderegg

Michael Anderegg, professor of English at the University of North Dakota, is the author of Orson Welles, Shakespeare, and Popular Culture.

In the following viewpoint, Anderegg describes a variety of interpretations and performances of Julius Caesar *in the twentieth century. He highlights perhaps the most famous of them all: Orson Welles's 1937 stage production subtitled* Death of a Dictator. *Four years before the United States entered World War II, Welles's version characterized Caesar as a fascist dictator, reflective of Germany's Adolf Hitler and especially Italy's Benito Mussolini. Twentieth-century literary critics of the play have generally taken the opposite view—defending Caesar and damning Brutus. Although Welles's* Julius Caesar *is the best known, other antifascist productions preceded it around the world. Still other productions have glorified Caesar in order to promote fascism, presenting Caesar's murder as a "historical catastrophe." Political adaptations for stage and film continue to be produced.*

"On 6 November 1937, at his fledging Mercury Theatre, [film director, writer, and actor] Orson Welles dragged *Caesar* [*Julius Caesar*] with traumatic abruptness into the twentieth century, accompanied by a degree of controversy unknown in its history." So [scholar] John Ripley writes in his otherwise sober *"Julius Caesar" on Stage.* The somewhat overheated tone is worthy of Welles himself, but Ripley's assessment is not far off the mark. Few productions of a [William] Shakespeare play have aroused as much interest, and have been as well remembered, as the so-called "Fascist" *Julius Caesar*. Set on "a bare stage, the brick walls of which are crimson and naked," emphasizing to the full the sculptural as well as melodramatic possibilities of lighting, and employing carefully choreographed crowd movement, the production was seen as "pure theatre; vibrant, unashamed and enormously effective." Although best remembered for its "Fascist" accouterments— modern military uniforms, straight-armed salutes, "Nuremberg" lighting—Welles's *Caesar* was at least as notable for the speed and simplicity of its staging, which brought to mind the "format of a radio or film script with episodes fading one into another, punctuated only by light, darkness, and sound effects."

An Antidictatorship Production

Welles's *Caesar*—subtitled *Death of a Dictator*—impressed critics and audiences of the time for its combination of a stylized simplicity and a thrilling evocation of contemporary political realities. The two worked in tandem—a modernist anti-realism combined with an urgency that grew out of the "Living Newspaper" format of the [Great Depression era] Works Progress Administration's Federal Theater, resulting in a style "compact, authoritative, fluid, and enormously absorbing." "Shakespeare has written so timely and provocative a piece"— [journalist] Heywood Broun wrote in *The New Republic*— "that the critics were actually arguing whether he favored fascism or communism or was perhaps a Trotskyite [a follower of Russian communist leader Leon Trotsky]." But, according to [writer and critic] Joseph Wood Krutch, "there is no forcing of the parallel and no distortion of Shakespeare's play to point a modern moral. . . . If this 'Julius Caesar' is not precisely that of the Elizabethans it emphasizes nothing which any modern reader of the play could well avoid seeing in it."

"The tragedy of the Globe Theatre across the Thames," [American theater critic] Brooks Atkinson wrote, "becomes the melodramatic tragedy of modern times just a few doors east of Broadway."

The Mercury production, as several of the reviewers were quick to note, thoroughly streamlined and simplified Shakespeare's play. Welles virtually eliminated two of the five acts, creating a more or less modern play on the bare skeletal outline of his original. He re-arranged scenes and altered the identity of speakers. The second movement of the play, the revenge of Caesar, was, perhaps necessarily, curtailed in a production that stressed the evils of dictatorship. . . .

[T]he brief scene in which the poet Cinna is mistaken for the conspirator with the same name, traditionally omitted in nineteenth- and early twentieth-century productions, became the highlight of the Mercury *Caesar*. In the words of one critic, "Not even the Group Theater in all their frenzy against dictators ever devised a more overwhelming scene than that in which the poet, Cinna, is swallowed up by an angry mob." Norman Lloyd, who played Cinna, has well described the effect: "I played a very gentle, diffident man with a great deal of pantomimic comedy; the terror came out of the comedy, which becomes very moving in the theatre." Unable to convince his listeners that he is not Cinna the conspirator, he is pressed all around by the mob. "As the gang surrounded me, I disappeared from the view of the audience save for one raised hand, with one last scream, 'The Poet!' The mob rushed me down the ramp at the back of the set out of sight of the audience, as if I were being devoured by an animal." "[F]or power and sinister meaning," Grenville Vernon wrote, this scene "has never been surpassed in the American theatre."

The Significance of Setting

The Mercury *Caesar* drew its most immediate inspiration from the political events taking place in Germany, Italy, Spain, and, indeed, much of Europe, but it would not have been possible without specific theatrical models as well. Welles and his partner John Houseman only had to look at the production of *Julius Caesar in Modern Clothes* staged months earlier by the Delaware Federal Theatre. Although in no way as imaginative as the Mercury production—the Fascist parallels appear to have been primarily a matter of costuming; the text followed nineteenth century promptbook traditions—this was probably the first production of the play to make unambiguous connections between Rome and contemporary Italy. "[A]s far as is known," the critic for the *Wilmington Morning News* observed, "this presentation of 'Julius Caesar' is the first of its kind since the days of Shakespeare, when all plays, historic or not, were costumed in the ordinary garb of the times." If this were not inspiration enough, the playwright Sidney Howard, in a letter to Houseman dated 9 February 1937, had suggested that the Mercury stage *Julius Caesar* as a modern play about Fascism. . . .

More recently, the critical tendency has been to denigrate Welles's production. "Modern attempts to confront [. . . *Julius Caesar*] have sometimes taken it away from Rome," David Daniell writes in the [1998] Arden Edition of the play, "as if the only way now to make sense of it were to make Caesar a modern Fascist dictator and Brutus and Cassius the leaders of a popular front . . . such simplification offers us Shakespeare's play shorn of mysteries and resonances." Comments like these partly disguise an unease with any interpretation of *Julius Caesar* critical of its titular figure. Whereas the stage history of *Julius Caesar*, particularly in nineteenth century America, has generally favored Brutus over Caesar, taking the former very much at his own valuation, the critical history of the play in the twentieth century has been governed by an essentially conservative point of view. While paying lip service to the belief that Shakespeare did not take sides in his delineation of the major characters (itself a dubious proposition), editors and critics often find it necessary to downgrade Brutus and puff up Caesar at every opportunity. Daniell, for example, provides the reader of his Arden text with a running discourse on the virtues of Caesar and the weakness, perfidy, and folly of Brutus. Daniell even undercuts Brutus's memorable "There is a tide in the affairs of men" speech, describing it as "a sermon on a worn adage about opportunity" which Brutus makes stand "for practical and detailed discussion with Cassius." Shakespeare, evidently, needs considerable help in making his (conservative) politics clear.

A "Fascist" setting, in any case, does not necessarily simplify the complexities of Shakespeare's play. Welles's production, as much as it may have employed [Adolf] Hitler and Albert Speer's "Nuremberg" lighting, is clearly meant to allude to Italian Fascism—we are still in Rome, Caesar is, more or less, [Benito] Mussolini, and Mussolini is not Hitler. In 1937, even a progressive would have been able to make distinctions between Hitler, [Francisco] Franco, and Mussolini. Welles's casting of Joseph Holland as Caesar, and the manner in which Holland performed the role, was intended to remind audiences of Il Duce, a man with very human, larger than life virtues (like personal courage) and flaws. Whatever we may think of Mussolini today, in the mid-1930s he was still capable of appealing to a range of political sensibilities. There was, at the very least, an ambiguity about his character and motives that provides a convincing analogy to Shakespeare's portrait of Caesar, a figure at once noble and ridiculous, vainglorious and brave. To have made Caesar into Hitler would have made nonsense of Shakespeare's play; to make Caesar resemble Mussolini is another thing altogether.

Caesar for the Fascist Agenda

Although Welles's Mercury production has come to be known as the "Fascist" *Julius Caesar*, a genuinely Fascist *Caesar* was produced at the Staatstheater in Berlin in 1941, directed by

Jürgen Fehling and starring, in the title role, the brilliant and notorious Werner Krauss, who that same year appeared in *Jud Süss*, "one of the most vicious anti-Semitic films ever made." Recent research has shown that Nazi theater, for a variety of interconnected reasons, was freer from official interference than might have been expected. One would nevertheless think that *Julius Caesar* was a dangerous play to put on in a dictatorship. Under the circumstances, it is not surprising to learn that Fehling did "everything in his power to enhance the role of Caesar and mark him out as the man of the future." Caesar's fall, in this production, was a "historical catastrophe, and his murder a crime of mythic proportion." Brutus lacked conviction, and failed "deservedly because of his adherence to dead ideas of liberal individualism comparable to the ones that had been current in the Weimar republic," whereas Mark Antony was "the warm, open-hearted friend, unsuspecting and generous, dragged into politics almost against his will but, once involved, an unstoppable force." Certainly, "[I]t would be difficult to claim that such a production was an invitation to tyrannicide," and yet one cannot help but wonder if audiences would have seen only what Fehling intended them to see.

The theatrical history of *Julius Caesar* subsequent to World War II has inevitably reverberated with echoes of the Mercury production. Though directors would not necessarily follow Welles's lead in constructing a specific Fascist context, few *Caesar*s would be entirely free of the ghost of Mussolini. Almost any modern-dress production could be seen as alluding to the Mercury *Caesar*, of course. One of the first to follow Welles's chronologically was staged in 1930s costuming in May of 1938 at the Festival Theatre, Cambridge; according to John Ripley, however, "there was no overt attempt to force a contemporary political parallel." Interestingly, both the first British (BBC, 24 July 1938) and the first U.S. (CBS, 12 March 1949) television productions of *Julius Caesar* were in modern dress, perhaps a bow to the modernity of television itself. The

BBC production directly alluded to Welles's, Italian uniforms and all, with some more elaborate updatings: "In the battle scenes, tanks, gas-masks, and dugouts were commonplace; and revolvers served as the instruments of death." . . .

The Televised Villains and Staged Dictators

The CBS "Studio One" *Caesar*, produced by Worthington Miner, reminded Jack Gould, the *New York Times* television critic, of "the memorable Orson Welles modernization." "In each case," Gould noted, "the text was edited to a swiftly moving documentary on revolution that none the less retained its substance as a social document and theatre classic." Military uniforms, Fascist salutes, and modern street clothes highlighted the production's *mise en scene*. Although some of [the] directorial touches may have been crude—after Antony describes Brutus as "the noblest Roman of them all," the camera reveals his foot, rolling Brutus's body into the street—the production as a whole, fusing "movement, word and lighting into a creative imagery that vividly thrust [the] audience into the midst of the turmoil in Rome," was a notable one in the history of televised Shakespeare.

Directors continue to modernize *Julius Caesar* without necessarily invoking 1930s style Fascism. A number of American productions have provided exotic locales and more or less modern dress as ways to bring *Julius Caesar* up-to-date: Latin America both at the Guthrie Theatre in Minneapolis in 1969 and at Stratford, Connecticut, in 1979; a specifically Cuban setting at the Oregon Shakespeare Festival in 1982. Several notable British productions have modernized the play through generalized reference to twentieth-century totalitarianism. Trevor Nunn's 1972 Royal Shakespeare Company's *Caesar* was set in a police state, complete with raised-arm salutes and "black-armoured soldiers to enforce the law," and a monumental statue of Caesar (an effect prefigured in the 1936 Prague production). Mark Dignam played Caesar, the *Financial*

Times reviewer noted, like "some timeless Mussolini." At least one observer felt that the Fascistic accouterments effectively overwhelmed "the hidden nuances of the text."

One of the more notable *Caesar*s in the last few decades was David Thacker's modern-dress promenade production staged at Stratford's Other Place in 1992. "Without employing all the available paraphernalia of modern politics and communications," [professor of Shakespeare studies] Russell Jackson observed, "the production superimposed the archetypal patterns of the play's fable on a recognizably modern political world." [Shakespeare scholar] Peter Holland's "hesitations about the production's contemporaneity" (Caesar was made up and costumed to resemble Boris Yeltsin [first president of the Russian Federation]) echoed the reservations of some critics about the Mercury *Caesar*: "if *Julius Caesar* celebrates, as we are celebrating, the overthrow of dictatorships like those of Eastern Europe, it is also a play far more uneasy about the manipulability of the mass of the people than I would like [it] to be. . . ."

A Political Play by Nature

Shakespeare's *Julius Caesar* is, almost to the exclusion of any other categorical description, a political play. As such, it necessarily opens itself to theatrical interpretations that may have little or nothing to do with either the specifics of pre-imperial Roman history or the politics of the Elizabethan monarchy. Though no production of *Julius Caesar* has, to my knowledge, aroused the same kinds of passions as have several productions of the more inflammatory *Coriolanus* [one of Shakespeare's two other Roman plays] playgoers, readers, directors, and critics could hardly ignore the words spoken by Cassius after the assassination of Caesar: "How many ages hence / Shall this our lofty scene be acted over / In states unborn and accents yet unknown?" Shakespeare may here be thinking as much of the hoped-for theatrical afterlife of his play as of the fall of tyrants, but his words certainly invite future audiences to seek for parallels in the political turmoil of their own times. The Mercury *Caesar*, both in itself and for the effect it has had on subsequent productions of Shakespeare's play, remains one of the most compelling and timely responses to that invitation.

Contemporary
Perspectives on Tyranny

Iran Elects a Radical, Unpredictable Leader: Mahmoud Ahmadinejad

Kasra Naji

Kasra Naji worked as a journalist in Tehran, Iran's capital, and has published articles in the Financial Times, *the* Guardian, *and the* Los Angeles Times, *among other publications.*

Mahmoud Ahmadinejad was elected president of Iran in August 2005 on the promise of a new revolution—bringing economic reforms to the poor and restoring an extremist Islamic state. According to Naji in this viewpoint, Ahmadinejad immediately moved to make himself known and disliked by many nations who fear his openly neo-Nazi position and his ambitions to create a nuclear bomb. Like Julius Caesar's, his base at first was the poor and his enemies were members of the establishment, whom he purged from his government. Yet he considers himself a divine leader appointed by Allah, and his regime is oppressive and extreme, claims Naji. In his fierce anti-Israeli stance, Ahmadinejad announced that the Holocaust never happened. His policies to improve the lives of the poor ended in economic disaster. And in Naji's view, his efforts to rid Iran of anything he considered incompatible with extreme Islam resulted in severe censorship and widespread rebellion, especially among students and teachers.

Within a year of his presidency [which began in 2005], [Mahmoud] Ahmadinejad had dragged Iran up the international agenda and raised his personal profile to within a hair's breadth of that of Ayatollah Khomeini [religious leader and politician]. His U-turn on reform, his strident anti-Israel

Kasra Naji, "Chapter 7: Iran in Turmoil," in *Ahmadinejad: The Secret History of Iran's Radical Leader*. Berkeley: University of California Press, 2008. Copyright © 2008 University of California Press (Books). All rights reserved. Reproduced by permission.

rhetoric and his aggressive resistance to US and UN [United Nations] pressure to halt Iran's nuclear programme had all won Ahmadinejad a place on the world stage. Somehow he had strengthened his domestic standing with people all across the political spectrum. He had isolated his critics and won the respect of the Muslim world.

Yet here was also a man who wrote incoherent letters to heads of state, who invited neo-Nazis to speak at high-profile events, who was lampooned and ridiculed the world over for believing that he was an agent of the divine, preparing Iran for the arrival of the messianic Missing Imam [religious leader]. Here was a leader whose grasp of geopolitics was rudimentary, a man who seemed not to understand economics, a man who would drag Iran to the brink of an unwinnable war with the West.

Intentionally, or not, Ahmadinejad's erratic and sensationalist behaviour had won him considerable global media attention. With his controversial views on the Holocaust and determination to press forward with the nuclear programme, every newspaper and news channel hung on his every pronouncement, no matter how unusual. CNN International and BBC World, as well as the Arabic channel Al Jazeera, took to broadcasting live portions of Ahmadinejad's frequent speeches on his visits to provincial towns in Iran. Even the most innocuous speech could yield the most amazing insights into this enigmatic world leader. On one occasion, BBC World even opted for the live transmission of Ahmadinejad's press conference in Tehran [Iran's capital] in preference to British prime minister Tony Blair's, which had been scheduled to take place more or less at the same time in London.

Ahmadinejad's poster appeared on the streets of several European capitals on billboards, advertising the news programmes of major television channels. He was the pin-up of political unrest. *Time* magazine was considering him for Person of the Year and sent a top photographer to do a session with the president in case he was chosen from the list of 26 candidates. Only two other Iranians had been *Time*'s person of the year: Ayatollah Khomeini in 1979 and Iran's fiercely nationalist prime minister Mohammad Mosaddeq in 1952. Ahmadinejad was increasingly viewing himself as the third great revolutionary leader of Iran, after the father of the modern nation, Mosaddeq, and the founder of the Islamic Republic, Khomeini. Somehow he simply was not bothered that this renown was earned for the wrong reasons. Ahmadinejad believed he had begun a new move in the world towards spiritualism. In his way of thinking, attacks on him in the Western media were just a sign that he was on the right track. If you didn't provoke the ire of your enemy, then surely you were doing something wrong.

A High Profile Leader

In the Arab world he was seen as an unambiguous hero, enjoying a standing comparable to that of some of the most popular Arab leaders in history, such as the Egyptian nationalist leader Gamal Abdel Nasser. Many in the Muslim world took great pride in the Iranian president and loved him as a no-nonsense leader standing up to the bullying Western powers. Even taxi drivers in Beijing liked him for his ordinary appearance and his perceived resistance to US imperialism. Because of this, Ahmadinejad was riding high at home. He continued to enjoy the support of the Supreme Leader, Ayatollah Khamenei, and, through the Ayatollah, he had the backing of the clergy, the judiciary and the whole religious conservative establishment. Pro-government newspapers and state-run television loved the exposure Ahmadinejad and Iran were getting, portraying it as a reflection of the power of Iran in the world under its down-to-earth president. The hardliners seized on the international attention Iran was getting to argue that Ahmadinejad had 'checkmated' Iran's enemies—the US, Britain, and all of the West—with his unwavering stances on

Mahmoud Ahmadinejad, elected president of Iran in 2005, considers himself a divine leader. AP Images/Wide Word Photos.

the Holocaust and the nuclear issue. As Ahmadinejad had expected, some doubters in the hardline camp joined him as he consolidated his power base.

Ahmadinejad was also careful not to forget his election goldmine: the rural poor. His provincial tours had became popular with locals, while a series of policies to help the poor won him a good deal of support across sections of the country generally ignored by Tehran. The provincial tours were also the ideal arena in which to try out his even more radical opinions and policies. High on his own success and popularity, and driven by a heartfelt zeal, Ahmadinejad wanted to rekindle the flames of the Revolution and return to the values of the early years. He began to speak openly on his tours of his ambition to unleash the Third Revolution. He travelled to small provincial towns and tried to engage with rural Iran, to understand and attend to their problems. All the while, he adopted a revolutionary persona in the mould of Ayatollah Khomeini in the early days of the Revolution. His language also changed to appeal better to the poor masses in provincial towns. He often used Khomeini-type language, simple but ferocious rhetoric, to denounce the US and Iran's other enemies, criticizing their opposition to Iran's nuclear activities. He championed the cause of Iran's right to nuclear technology. The crowds loved it when he prompted them to shout 'Nuclear energy is our legitimate right'. Deep down, the president was a rabble rouser. In the current climate, it seemed to be politically expedient but, more than that, he positively enjoyed it. . . .

The Third Revolution

Six months into his term of office Ahmadinejad had created enough uncertainties to plunge the country into chaos and turmoil. But, he believed, that was the price to be paid for a genuine and far-reaching revolution—the Third Revolution. In Ahmadinejad's words, the new revolution aimed to change the country's power structure in favour of social justice at home. He also aspired to bring peace and equality to the entire world—and he really meant it. As he repeatedly made clear, the president believed that he was divinely appointed to prepare both Iran and the whole world for the imminent return of the Mahdi [the redeemer of Islam]. The Mahdi was to bring about a new global regime of peace and justice, and Ahmadinejad was driven by the belief that his policies and actions would make the Mahdi's task easy once he arrived. 'The Third Revolution has begun. It will revolutionize relations among the people, between the management of the country and the people, and among the managers,' he said after his election as president. In the Iranian revolutionary vocabulary, the first revolution was the Islamic Revolution of 1979 that overthrew the monarchy. The Second Revolution, so designated by Ayatollah Khomeini, referred to the occupation of the US embassy in Tehran, the event which led Iran to turn away from the West.

Now it was time for the Third Revolution. But what exactly did that mean? Ahmadinejad had used the phrase throughout his election campaign and with greater frequency since coming to power. During the campaign, he had explained that the Third Revolution would aim to rid the country of liberal and secular influences and establish a truly Islamic government. 'Today we have managers in the country who do not believe in the ability of Islam to administer society, managers who approve of liberal ideas, managers who believe in progress only in the framework of individualistic, material and secular initiatives, managers who lack confidence in their own Islamic culture when confronting the cultural onslaught of the West. These managers are weak in front of the enemies and look down on their own people.' He said the Islamic Revolution had failed to eradicate poverty, corruption and discrimination. 'Unfortunately we are still facing moral as well as political and administrative corruption.' . . .

Ahmadinejad Confronts the Ruling Elite and Democracy

There can be no doubt that from the very day he took power Ahmadinejad was committed to inspiring the Iranian people to rise up against the status quo, both nationally and internationally. 'A huge energy has been released in our country and we must put this to good use,' he said. But who were the president's targets, and why?

Internationally, the issue was simple. Ahmadinejad wanted a fundamental change in international relations, particularly at the UN where the five powers with the right of veto had disproportionate control and authority over other countries. But if Ahmadinejad was shouting about 'one member one vote' at the UN, he sang a very different tune domestically. Within Iran, the key target of the Third Revolution was the ruling elite and their ideology of democratic Islam. Ahmadinejad's election had handed the government to the Islamic neo-conservatives. Together with their allies in the Revolutionary Guard and the Basij, this faction wanted—as a first step—to purge the government and the bureaucracy of the reformists who spoke of democracy, the rule of law and the establishment of civil society. These were seen as un-Islamic and therefore unacceptable.

Professor Fred Halliday of the London School of Economics has described what had been happening in Iran with the election of Ahmadinejad as 'a revolutionary spasm', not dissimilar to the symptoms suffered by many other revolutions. 'In a crucial respect, this revolution, like many other upheavals, is moving after twenty years, not into a "reform" phase, but into a "twenty-year spasm"—a second reassertion of militancy and egalitarianism that rejects domestic elites and external pressure alike (as in Russia in the purge era of the late 1930s, China under the "cultural revolution" of the late 1960s, and Cuba in the "rectification" campaign of the 1980s). In Ahmadinejad's revolution, the wrath of the people should not be directed against the Supreme Leader, and he was very firm in his distinction between the glorious, inspired, revolutionary Islamic leaders and the corrupt, ineffective, bureaucratic, un-Islamic managers of government. 'We have to make the people understand ... that the problems, the weaknesses and the deviations have nothing to do with the leader of the Revolution and the regime. They are the making of managers who have deviated from the Revolution.' One target of his 'revolution' was none other than his old rival in the presidential elections—[Ayatollah] Rafsanjani and his allies. That Rafsanjani had strong revolutionary credentials did not stop Ahmadinejad smearing his political record and his private character. 'In an Islamic government we cannot have someone who is involved in gigantic economic deals taking the reins of the government or being present in the management of the country,' he said in an obvious dig at Rafsanjani, who had reputedly amassed considerable wealth for himself and whose sons were commercially highly active.

Over the first two years of Ahmadinejad's presidency, the expression 'Third Revolution' gradually gave way to references to 'a second wave of the revolution'. Perhaps this was to emphasize that what was taking place was a direct continuance of the events of 1979 and 1980. Also, while a Third Revolution might be expected to have some clear, achievable goals and to occur within a delineated time-frame, a 'second wave' was a more nebulous concept and more open to interpretation and extension. Central to the Ahmadinejad revolution was a dogged and violent pursuit of his own ideals and morality, without bowing to anyone else.

Throughout this time the Supreme Leader remained silent on the return of the Revolution. Many believed that he had privately given Ahmadinejad the go-ahead for his revolution and that it might even have been Khamenei's idea. Certainly it appeared that the Ayatollah was supportive of a huge purge and a fresh start in Iran. But to do this, Ahmadinejad needed more than cheering and waving from the populace. He needed an Iranian people energized and committed to his vision of the new Iran. . . .

The president began Iran's second Cultural Revolution at Tehran University—the oldest and one of the most prestigious universities in Iran. First, he appointed a clergyman as chancellor, Ayatollah Abbas Ali Amid Zanjani—the first ever cleric to become chancellor of an Iranian university. Predictably, this appointment was met with student protests but these were stone-walled. Ahmadinejad decided that he needed to move slowly against the universities, which still commanded considerable respect as the political conscience of the nation.

Objections to the Dictator

A few months after the controversial appointment of Zanjani, Ahmadinejad gave a speech to another university in Tehran, the Amir Kabir University. At Amir Kabir, the students noisily rejected him as a dictator and a fascist. Although the auditorium had been filled with student members of the Basij militia from many universities, dozens of Amir Kabir students managed to get in. Time and again, they drowned out the voice of Ahmadinejad with their shouts of 'dictator' and 'fascist'. Ahmadinejad tried to make the best of the situation by raising his own voice and appearing calm and unfazed. But the students simply raised the temperature. Rising from their seats, they held his posters upside down—a strong mark of disrespect—and some even set fire to them. Others threw firecrackers at the stage, but the president's security men remained calm. The Amir Kabir protest was taking place at the same time as the notorious Holocaust-denial conference, and the students took the opportunity to express their disgust, with placards clearly branding the president a friend of neo-Nazis.

The Amir Kabir demonstration might only have comprised several dozen students but it was a significant event and the first public protest against Ahmadinejad since his taking office nearly 18 months earlier. The students believed that they had sent a strong message to the president: do not mess with the universities. With cheeky boldness, Ahmadinejad even tried to represent the protest as a proud testament to the political and personal freedoms of Iran, claiming in his weblog that the sight of 'a small group who against a massive majority dared to insult the president in full freedom' made him proud that the Islamic Revolution had brought such freedoms to the nation. Ahmadinejad went further and promised that the students would not be persecuted for what they had done. But it was a hollow promise. Reprisals would come but only after the furore had died down and would be conducted through indirect channels. Many of the students were later harassed, beaten, jailed and expelled from the university. A few were sent on military service.

A Cuban Leader's Vulnerable Relationship with His People: Fidel Castro

Daniel P. Erikson

Daniel Erikson is a senior associate for US policy at the Inter-American think tank in Washington, D.C., and has published more than fifty essays in major newspapers.

In 1959 Fidel Castro seized power from Fulgencio Batista, a capitalist dictator known for corruption and the exploitation of Cuba's resources. Castro's communist regime operated under the image of "defender of the downtrodden and dispossessed" and in Castro's view, it provided excellent systems of health, education, and energy. According to Erikson in this viewpoint, even at the age of eighty, Castro remained the strong absolute dictator of his country who claimed never to have made a dollar for his own personal benefit. Yet Castro was despised and experienced numerous assassination attempts, says Erikson, often on trips to other Latin American countries—even though, paradoxically, he was considered to be a world hero, "a rock star," in much of South and Central America. Despite his alleged reforms, states Erikson, Castro still behaved as a tyrant, cultivating a police state and punishing dissidents. Castro's hypocritical practices stirred hidden hatred for him in his own country.

Fidel Castro [president of Cuba] was accustomed to keeping his country immersed in a state of feverish speculation, but now the time for a decision loomed. Nearly nineteen months had passed while he tried to battle back from the illness that had forced him to relinquish power in July 2006. His

Daniel P. Erikson, "Chapter 1: Die Another Day," in *The Cuba Wars: Fidel Castro, the United States, and the Next Revolution*. Bloomsbury Press, 2008. Copyright © 2008 Bloomsbury Publishing plc.

health had collapsed during the early months, leaving him at death's door, but he had been gradually gaining strength and weight, and it was possible that he would live for some time more. His brother Raúl, who had assumed the provisional powers of government in Fidel's absence, had proved to be a competent administrator, but he was also growing restless. Moreover, Fidel was aware that his precarious health had ushered his nation into a strange twilight zone that had left him at the mercy of his successors, not the other way around.

Fidel had not been seen publicly in Cuba since his health crisis began, but he remained a prominent voice by writing periodic "reflections" in the national press about international issues that grabbed his attention. . . .

Conflicting Emotions Over a Revolutionary

"I die just about every day," Fidel Castro told a television interviewer several weeks before reaching his eightieth birthday in 2006. "But it's really a lot of fun for me, and it makes me feel healthier." Indeed, the aging bearded leader who had ruled Cuba for decades appeared to be in fighting form during that long, hot summer. Hundreds of thousands of Cubans gathered in Havana's Plaza of the Revolution to see him speak at the country's annual May Day celebrations, where he peppered his remarks with statistics about Cuba's health, education, and energy programs and sarcastically thanked the United States for its long-standing embargo of Cuba. After more than forty-seven years in power, Castro still provoked deep and conflicting emotions within the Cuban population, where he was adored, feared, and despised—sometimes all at once. But no one doubted that he remained fully in charge of his country, a picturesque island just off the coast of the United States that was one of the world's last remaining communist regimes.

Castro loved to bask in the limelight, and controversy followed him throughout the spring and summer. In May, he became entangled in a surreal sparring match with *Forbes* magazine, which featured him in a special survey of the world's richest "Kings, Queens and Dictators" and ranked him as the seventh richest, with an estimated wealth of nine hundred million dollars, nearly double the estimated wealth of the queen of England. The claim sent Castro into a state of apoplexy, prompting him to make a special appearance on Cuban television in which he pounded the table and denounced his presence on the *Forbes* list as "repugnant slander." The magazine admitted its back-of-the-envelope calculations were "more art than science," but Castro was incensed. Accusations of illicit wealth threatened to undermine his carefully cultivated image as an international defender of the downtrodden and dispossessed, and he dismissed the *Forbes* statistic as a smear campaign engineered by the [George W.] Bush administration and the Central Intelligence Agency. Castro then issued a challenge: "If they can prove that I have one single dollar, I will resign from all my responsibilities and the duties I am carrying out. They won't need any more plans of transitions!"

Assassination Plots Against Castro

In July, Castro remained an active force in Cuba, presiding over high-level government discussions, approving a series of new joint ventures with Canadian and Spanish companies, and overseeing plans to celebrate his eightieth birthday on August 13. Toward the end of the month, Castro made a snap decision to attend a South American summit meeting in Argentina at the invitation of his close friend and ally Hugo Chávez [president of Venezuela]. Castro always enjoyed the element of surprise, and it was his custom to leave his travel plans unannounced until the last minute, in part for security reasons. Some of the most brazen assassination attempts against him had occurred at international gatherings in Latin America, and this trip marked his first overseas venture since a short visit to Barbados the previous December.

Besides, Castro was a popular figure in Argentina, a country still suffering from the scars of a brutal economic collapse in 2001 triggered in part by the "neoliberal" economic policies that the Cuban leader never tired of railing against. Castro had been greeted like a rock star during a visit three years earlier, and cries of "Viva Fidel!" followed him as he arrived in the country anew on July 21. "Sometimes I have to misinform even my own friends. Not even I knew I was going to come," he told a crowd at an "anti-imperialist" rally in Argentina's second city, Córdoba. He joined with Hugo Chávez the next day to visit the boyhood home of Ernesto "Che" Guevara, the Argentine medical student who went on to become one of the most iconic figures of the Cuban Revolution. It was an emotional event for the two leaders, especially Chávez, who explained, "Fidel invited me to come and get to know the house. For me, it's a real honor being here." Their celebrity tour left some nearby neighbors reeling from the experience, including one Argentine housewife who commented that the uproar "has thrown the whole city into a state of shock."

An Example of Tyrannical Behavior

Castro's Argentine tour ended on a sour note, however, when an enterprising journalist provoked him into an angry tirade by asking about a sensitive case involving one of Cuba's most noted dissidents. Hilda Molina was one of Cuba's top neurosurgeons and had been a medical superstar until the island's economy started to unravel following the collapse of the Soviet Union in the early 1990s. During the resulting crisis, Cuban medical care facilities were ordered to turn away needy Cubans and instead set aside beds for foreign patients who could pay in hard currency. Molina protested the new policies, which ended her glittering career in the communist system. In 1994, her son fled abroad to Argentina, but the Cuban government refused to allow her to leave, arguing that "your brain is the patrimony of the nation." Molina was unable to even meet her grandchildren, who were later born in Argentina, a situation she decried as "supreme cruelty." The plight of a grandmother separated from her grandchildren turned the case into a cause célèbre, and Argentine president Néstor Kirchner had repeatedly tried to use his cordial relationship with Castro to help Molina gain her coveted exit visa, to no avail.

In Argentina, Juan Manuel Cao, a Cuban American television reporter from Miami, dogged the official Cuban delegation with questions about Molina. When Castro joined the South American presidents at the summit for an official photo ceremony, the scene consisted of barely constrained chaos as photographers, journalists, and spectators jockeyed for the best view of the Cuban leader. Sensing his opportunity, the Miami reporter cried out to Castro, "Why don't you free Dr. Hilda Molina? Why don't you let her come see her grandchildren?" Fidel Castro immediately fixated on the journalist, asking, "What's your name? Who is paying you to come and ask questions like this?" The reporter volunteered that he was from Cuba, and Castro nearly flipped with rage. "I already asked you who paid you," he shouted. "Why don't you look for Bush and ask him about Posada Carriles and the crimes they have committed in his country? Cuban?! You are not Cuban. Che is Cuban. You are an intruder that is living like a mercenary. That's what you are." Most of the exchange was captured on videotape, with photographers' flashbulbs erupting in rapid succession. The stray question had clearly provoked Castro. The fearsome Cuban dictator was getting pretty thin-skinned in his old age.

Castro's Earlier Overthrow of a Capitalist Dictator

Castro arrived back in Havana on July 23, and several days later he traveled down to Bayamo, a sleepy provincial capital located about seventy miles west of Santiago de Cuba, his hometown and the city where his initial assault on the established order of Cuba unfolded on July 26, 1953. On that date, Castro led a group of 150 rebels in a surprise attack on a military garrison in Santiago with the intention of igniting a movement to unseat the dictatorship of Fulgencio Batista. The attack was a military debacle that resulted in the deaths of dozens of rebels, but it succeeded in launching Castro as a major national figure at the tender age of twenty-six, and he later defended himself in a famous speech titled "History Will Absolve Me." He spent nearly two years in a Cuban prison before winning early release in 1955 and leaving for exile in Mexico, and in December 1956, he captained a barely seaworthy vessel named the *Granma* from Mexico to the southern shore of Cuba to relaunch the revolution that would eventually bring him to power on January 1, 1959. Castro christened his revolutionary organization the 26th of July Movement, in honor of the date that marked his first military excursion. As president, he made that date a national holiday in Cuba, and he commemorated it with a major speech annually. . . .

Hidden Views of Castro

Once I was on the edge of a plaza in Old Havana talking with two teenage boys about life in Cuba. It was several years before Castro fell ill, and his seemingly never-ending rule cast a long shadow over his country. "We can't wait until the old man goes," they told me. "Everything here needs to change." By sheer coincidence, an official convoy pulled up across the street in the middle of our conversation, and Castro stepped out of one of the vehicles. It was a spur-of-the-moment visit to a local school, and a crowd immediately surrounded him. The two teenagers pivoted—almost in mid-sentence—and began to chant, "Viva Fidel! Viva Fidel!" with a starstruck look in their eyes. Later I recounted this story to an older Cuban man from the generation that helped thrust Castro into the center of power. He told me, "It's true—he's a hero, but we hate him." When I suggested that he would probably cry on the day that Castro died, he smiled and murmured, "Of course I will. But they will be tears of joy."

Communist North Korea Becomes Increasingly Isolated: Kim Jong Il

Richard Worth

Richard Worth is an author of nonfiction, including the book Gangs and Crime.

In 1980 the leader of North Korea was chosen, not by the people or even by a parliament, but by the new leader's own father, who had been dictator before him. According to Worth in the viewpoint that follows, Kim Jong Il used terror tactics before and during his rule, including kidnapping citizens of other countries and imprisoning thousands. Among those he kidnapped and imprisoned were an actress and a film director he needed for a film project. While he was spending millions on his filmmaking and building up the military, Worth explains, the economy was becoming weaker and his people more destitute. Meanwhile North Korea's foreign policy decisions influenced broken alliances, and the nation found itself increasingly isolated under Kim Jong Il's leadership. Under these conditions North Korea began a nuclear weapons program, says Worth, in order to gain the attention and respect of the world's major powers.

In 1980, Kim Il Sung made an official announcement that his son, Kim Jong Il, would be his successor as head of the North Korean government. Meanwhile, the younger Kim had also become a secretary—that is, a leader—of the Communist Workers' Party. He was known as the Dear Leader to distinguish him from his father, the Great Leader. Portraits of the Dear Leader and the Great Leader appeared side by side inside government buildings in Pyongyang and throughout the rest of North Korea. The North Korean people also displayed pictures of both leaders in their homes.

Although Kim Jong Il had achieved enormous power in North Korea, he continued to work behind the scenes and did not show himself in public very much. He rarely met with foreign heads of state who came to North Korea, and he rarely traveled abroad. Kim Il Sung still served as the public leader of North Korea, but during much of the 1980s, his son was actually running the government. To prepare North Koreans for the day that Kim Jong Il would take over from his father, Communist officials began to build up the younger Kim's public image. A museum portraying his accomplishments had already been built in Pyongyang, but new elements of his life suddenly began to appear.

The Dear Leader's Bold Tactics

Meanwhile, Kim Jong Il was also trying to distinguish himself as a movie producer. Kim is a devoted movie fan, with thousands of films reportedly stored in his library. He was eager to increase North Korea's prestige by producing award-winning films. To help him accomplish this goal, Kim decided to bring a famous South Korean director, Shin Sang-ok, to the North. Kim's agents first kidnapped Shin's former wife, the highly successful actress Choi Eun-hi when she was visiting Hong Kong in 1978. After she arrived in Pyongyang, Kim gave her a beautiful home and an expensive car. Although Choi did not know why she had been kidnapped, it eventually became apparent to her. Shin, who had continued to be fond of his wife after their divorce, tried to find Choi after her disappearance. This led him to Hong Kong, where he was grabbed by North Korean agents. When he refused to remain in North Korea and tried to escape, Shin was jailed. Finally, he agreed to write a letter to Kim Jong Il apologizing for his conduct. Eventually, Shin was released, and in 1983, he was reunited with his former wife. Shin then went to work directing films in North Korea in a multimillion-dollar studio built by Kim. Shin and Choi were permitted to travel abroad to publicize the films. At first, they were heavily guarded, but when they convinced Kim of their loyalty, he removed the guards. In 1986, they escaped and never returned to North Korea.

Kim's Economic Mismanagement

While Kim spent millions on film production, the North Korean economy continued to lag during the 1980s. Instead of improving industrial production, a large amount of money was spent on building up the military. In addition, the North Korean government had focused much of its remaining resources on huge projects that failed. Among these was an expensive dam, called the West Sea Barrage, started in 1981 and finished five years later. The main purpose of the dam was to irrigate several hundred thousand acres of saltwater tidelands along the coast that were to be transformed into productive farms. This supported the government's chuch'e program leading to self-sufficiency in food production. But after the barrage was completed, the government never followed through on the plan to expand the nation's farmland, and very little tideland actually became productive farms.

Another plan called for the development of a new vinalon plant. Vinalon was a chemical fiber used to make clothing and shoes. Instead of cotton, which was difficult to grow in North Korea, the chuch'e program of self-sufficiency substituted vinalon. In the 1950s, this was produced from coal and limestone, both easily available in North Korea. The new plant called for even greater production. As by-products, the plant was also designed to produce large quantities of fertilizer and food for farm animals. But after the plant was begun at huge cost, it was never completed. A third very expensive project was a fertilizer complex, designed to increase crop production. But this complex also failed to be completed.

Meanwhile, food shortages in the North continued to grow during the 1980s. By this time, Kim Jong Il was directly in charge of the government, so he was blamed for the problem. Not only was grain and rice being rationed for Korean civilians, soldiers in the armed forces were also short of food. According to Lee Min-bok, a food expert who escaped from North Korea, the rationing grew much worse by the mid-1980s. People were supposed to receive food every two weeks at large distribution centers, but the rations frequently failed to arrive on time. . . .

A Façade of Prosperity

Nevertheless, the North Korean economy continued to struggle. In 1986, author Jasper Becker visited Pyongyang. As his car headed toward the capital, he noticed that the highway was almost empty of cars. There was too little gasoline to run them. The subway stations inside the city were bright and clean, but hardly ever used. "The inhabitants' chief role," he wrote, "is to take part in mass demonstrations of support, and they are constantly in training to perform at some military parade, celebration, or demonstration. . . . You find the same familiar sights as in any big city—department stores, grocery shops, smart hotels, bars, restaurants, and hospitals—but nothing as mundane as shopping or eating goes on in them. From the outside a grocery store looks normal. The windows and glass counters are clean and hygienic, the vegetables are in the baskets, the tins of meat on wooden shelves, and the condiment [spice] bottles are laid neatly in rows. Yet there is nobody there. No one is shopping, and no one ever will. Nothing is actually for sale because when you look closely the vegetables are all made of plastic. . . . On a tour of the maternity hospital, it is the same. The rooms, full of new, modern medical equipment, are for show too. Not even the plastic wrapping on the electrical plug for the . . . heart monitor has been removed."

Under the rule of Kim Jong Il, North Korea became increasingly isolated. AP Images/ Chien-Min Chung.

Kim's Brutal Practices

While he was dealing with the problems of North Korea's economy, Kim Jong Il was also running North Korea's foreign affairs. To show off the power of North Korea, Kim sent his agents to kidnap citizens of Japan and South Korea. These people were taken to prison camps in North Korea, where they disappeared. As a way of boosting its lagging economy, North Korea had also become a major supplier of arms to other nations, especially in the Middle East. These weapons included tanks, short-range missiles, and missile launchers to countries such as Iraq, Libya, and Syria.

In 1982, Kim had launched an assassination plot aimed at South Korea's president, Chun Doo Hwan. The following year, Chun and senior members of his government were visiting Rangoon, the capital of Burma (now called Myanmar). Some of them had already arrived for an official ceremony at the capital, but Chun was running behind schedule. As the South Korean officials prepared for Chun's arrival, a bomb suddenly exploded, killing four of them. The bomb had been planted by a North Korean army officer, Zin Mo, and several other agents. They were later caught and confessed that the bombing had been planned by the North Korean government.

President Chun and his U.S. allies feared that the assassinations might be followed by North Korean military action along the Demilitarized Zone. Indeed some members of the president's cabinet wanted to bomb North Korea. But Chun refused to allow any attack. Indeed, in 1984, secret talks had begun between North Korea and South Korea aimed at improving relations between the two countries. They were conducted by Park Chul Un, a South Korean diplomat and an expert in foreign affairs, and Han Se Hae, a leading North Korean diplomat.

The two men hoped to lay the foundation for a summit meeting between Kim Il Sung and Chun Doo Hwan. But there were too many disagreements between the two sides, and the secret talks finally ended. The North Korean government was especially upset by a military training exercise, called Team Spirit, that was scheduled for 1985. Kim Jong Il believed that this exercise, which involved thousands of U.S. and South Korean troops, posed a threat to his father's regime. . . .

Isolation Pushes North Korea to a New Strategy

On January 1, 1991, [Soviet leader Mikhail] Gorbachev established full diplomatic relations with South Korea. Up until this time, the USSR had recognized only North Korea as the legitimate government of the Korean Peninsula. Gorbachev's decision, combined with weakening economic conditions in the Soviet Union, changed the situation in North Korea. In the past, the Soviets had provided crucial oil supplies to North Korea as well as weapons and industrial machinery. These had been sold at specially reduced prices, and the Soviets had even allowed Kim not to pay for much of what he had received.

Suddenly, this special relationship had changed. Oil supplies to North Korea were reduced by 75 percent. Since part of the oil was used in chemical fertilizer, farm production was affected. Gasoline supplies were also reduced for tanks and airplanes. Kim Jong Il turned to China, which had also supplied North Korea with oil. But the Chinese refused to supply oil at the low prices offered in the past by the Soviets. When Don Oberdorfer visited North Korea in 1991, he noticed "deserted roadways and idle construction projects" around Pyongyang. There was no gasoline to run automobiles or heavy construction equipment.

In 1992, the Chinese also decided to establish diplomatic relations with South Korea. This decision, along with the changing policies in the Soviet Union, left Kim Jong Il and his father feeling more and more isolated in North Korea. As a result, they turned to a new strategy—one designed to get the attention of their former Communist allies as well as the rest of the world.

During the mid-1980s, North Korea had begun receiving nuclear reactors from the Soviet Union. These were designed to enable the development of nuclear power for generating electricity. At the same time, Moscow required Kim Il Sung to join the Nuclear Non-Proliferation Treaty. Begun in 1968, it committed the nations that signed the treaty to stop the spread of nuclear weapons. But while Pyongyang agreed to the terms of the treaty, it was secretly developing a nuclear weapons program. U.S. surveillance satellites had photographed the buildings involved in the program at Yongbyon, north of Pyongyang, as early as 1982. The nuclear facilities included a reactor, and a few years later, a partly completed reprocessing plant. This might have given the North Koreans the capability of separating plutonium from nuclear fuel and building an atomic bomb.

The nuclear weapons program was directed by Dr. Lee Sung Ki, a close friend of the Great Leader. Kim Il Sung and his son believed that as their economy declined a nuclear bomb might force the major world powers to pay attention to North Korea. This would put the Communist regime on an equal footing with the United States, China, and the USSR, each of which had nuclear capability. In addition, it would give North Korea the power to control events on the Korean Peninsula.

A Latin American Leader Becomes a Global Icon: Hugo Chávez

Moisés Naím

Moisés Naím, editor in chief of Foreign Policy *magazine, is the former minister for trade and industry of Venezuela.*

In the oil-rich country of Venezuela, President Hugo Chávez is classified by many as a benevolent dictator whose charity extends to the poor in other countries, even the United States. In the following viewpoint, Naím explains how distant audiences in India, Lebanon, and South Africa praised Chávez highly. The sympathy that he has garnered in his own country and throughout the world comes from his promise to fight corruption, inequality, and social injustice, asserts Naím. Although he has become an icon among the poor in Venezuela, Chávez has made many enemies there among the power elite, including political leaders, business leaders, labor leaders, and oil company executives. The author notes that Chávez was democratically elected; he did not use force to secure his reforms. Still critics claim that Chávez has bewitched his people and that he rigged his 2006 election. Naím believes that while Chávez has some admirable motives, his policies will ultimately harm Venezuela's economy and political freedoms.

Janetta Morton lives about a half hour away from the White House. Not that she has ever been there. The unemployed single mother of two girls shares a small house with her sister in one of the poorest neighborhoods in Washington, D.C. Morton does not know much about Hugo Chávez. But for

Moisés Naím, "Introduction," in *Hugo Chávez: The Definitive Biography of Venezuela's Controversial President*, ed. Cristina Marcano and Alberta Barrera Tyska, trans. Kristina Cordero. Copyright © 2007 by Moisés Naím. Used by permission of Random House, Inc.

her, the Venezuelan president is a hero. "I wish George W. Bush was like him," she says. Morton is one of the 1.2 million poor Americans who get discounted heating fuel for their homes from CITGO, an Oklahoma-based oil company owned by the Venezuelan government. She also got a glossy brochure explaining that this was just an act of basic human solidarity from a president that cares for the poor everywhere, not just in his native Venezuela. "This is not about politics," the brochure said.

Worldwide Admiration for Chávez

In South Africa, President Chávez also has admirers. In Soweto, a poor neighborhood in Johannesburg, political activists enthusiastically follow Chávez's Bolivarian Revolution, and some of them were invited to Venezuela to see it firsthand and even to meet with the president. They too say that they would like a leader like Hugo Chávez for their country. In Lebanon, some Hezbollah [Islamic political and paramilitary organization] supporters have named their newborn sons Hugo.

Andres Oppenheimer, a syndicated columnist for *The Miami Herald*, traveled to India in January 2007 to interview business leaders, politicians, and others about that nation's profound transformation. One of his stops offered quite a surprise. Reporting from New Delhi, Oppenheimer writes:

> I happened to be giving a talk at the Jawaharlal Nehru University here the day that Venezuelan President Hugo Chávez announced the nationalization of key industries. I thought the news would help me make the case that Chávez is destroying Venezuela's economy. How wrong I was!
>
> Far from applauding, the professors and students at the School of International Studies—a major recruiting ground for foreign service officials—were looking at me with a mixture of anthropological curiosity and disbelief. It was obvious that, for most of them, Chávez was a hero. . . .

"How many of you think Chávez is doing a lot of good for Venezuela?" I asked my audience. Most of the students raised their hands.

"Why do you think that?" I asked. A doctoral student named Jagpal, who is doing his thesis on Venezuela, said that Chávez had put an end to a corrupt economic and political elite, and had focused the government's attention on the poor.

Janetta Morton, the Soweto activists, the Lebanese parents, and the Indian university students are only four examples of a rare and far wider phenomenon: a Latin American political leader who becomes a household name and a global icon.

It is a rare phenomenon because Hugo Chávez is the only Latin American politician in the past half century who has been able to acquire the type of worldwide name recognition and star power enjoyed by [Cuban revolutionaries] Ernesto "Che" Guevara and Fidel Castro.

How did this happen? How did a poor boy, born and raised in Sabaneta, a small city deep inside Los Llanos ("the plains") of a country mostly known to the rest of the world for its oil and beauty queens, grow up to become almost as well known as—and far more admired than—the president of the United States [George W. Bush]? What does Hugo Chávez have that other leaders in Latin America or any other poor region in the world don't have?

Conditions of the President's Rise to Power

The answers to these questions provide interesting clues not just about Chávez the man; they also reveal interesting trends in the politics and economics of the world in the early years of the twenty-first century. . . .

Personal histories, as we know, are shaped by the places and times in which they occur. In an increasingly connected and interdependent world, they are also shaped by what is going on elsewhere. And sometimes "elsewhere" can be very far

Venezuelan president Hugo Chávez was democratically elected in 2006. AP Images/
Fernando Llano.

away. Afghanistan, for example, is very far from Venezuela. So
is Iraq. Yet Hugo Chávez's performance and possibilities are
closely intertwined with events in these places located at
Venezuela's antipodes or to the events in lower Manhattan on

September 11, 2001. For many reasons unrelated to Chávez, he turned out to be one of the main beneficiaries of the terrorist attacks of 9/11 against the United States. Not that he had anything to do with the attacks. But partly as a consequence of 9/11, oil prices more than doubled—and sent a tsunami of petrodollars to the coffers of the Venezuelan government.

Moreover, 9/11 also focused the American superpower almost exclusively on Islamic terrorism and on waging wars in faraway places. Leaders in the United States had no time to pay much attention to what was going on in their traditional geopolitical backyard, Latin America. Chávez deftly exploited this distraction. In addition, President George W. Bush's decisions, rhetoric, and demeanor boosted anti-American sentiments worldwide to levels that may well be unprecedented. The Venezuelan president was ready, even eager, to seize the moment and become the world's most strident critic of the U.S. president.

Chávez was not just well positioned—financially and politically—to take advantage of these global trends; he was also ready to boldly act on his instincts. He understood very quickly that the emperor had no clothes and that challenging the American "empire" and its internationally unpopular leader was a sure bet. He could afford the gamble thanks to the oil money that had made Venezuela less reliant on foreign investors, U.S. credits, or aid. President Chávez calculated that insulting the American president carried low risks and would yield huge political benefits at home and abroad. Not even [militant Islamist] Osama bin Laden or [former president of Iraq] Saddam Hussein had said in front of the cameras—or the United Nations—what the Venezuelan president says about George W. Bush. "Drunkard," "asshole," "coward," "thug," "assassin," "baby killer," and "genocidal war-criminal" are just some of the names that President Chávez regularly calls his American counterpart. Most of the world smiles and privately (and often not that privately) shares the negative feelings about one of the most disdained U.S. presidents in recent history. From Moscow to Malawi, the anti-Bush antics of Hugo Chávez are part of the regular fare of the evening news.

Chávez vs. the Aristocracy

But Hugo Chávez has not just been bold abroad; he has also been daring at home. There he detected another emperor who had no clothes: the traditional Venezuelan power elite. And, once again, he boldly acted on that instinct. He gambled on the possibility that the political parties, business conglomerates, media tycoons, oil-industry executives, and labor oligarchs that had called the shots for half a century in Venezuela were weak and vulnerable. He realized that the country's power structure was ready for a hostile takeover. Further he discovered that this takeover could be based on ballots, not bullets. And that in the twenty-first century in a country like Venezuela, democracy could be used to acquire enormous powers not afforded to democratically elected presidents elsewhere.

In the opinion of some, the almost dictatorial powers acquired by Hugo Chávez are being put to good use. He needs the power to redress the injustices wrought by centuries of abuse against the poor and the powerless. To others, this is not different from any other authoritarian episode in a region where they have been all too common.

So, is Hugo Chávez a democrat committed to helping the poor, or just an old-school, power-grabbing populist? Once again, in the answers to these questions lie interesting clues about larger trends in Latin America and elsewhere. But the answers, of course, depend not only on political and economic circumstances. They also depend on Chávez, the man. . . .

Hugo Chávez has harbored grand, enduring ambitions since he was a very young man. "One day I will be the president of this country," he told an incredulous friend during a road trip when they were both in their early twenties. ("I told him he was drunk," the friend recalls.). . . From a very young age, crude Communist ideas, plotting against "the system," and becoming "someone that really matters in this country" were permanent drivers of Chávez's behavior. These thoughts have not gone away. In fact, they have grown larger. For example, the now middle-aged president is obviously no longer satisfied to be someone who matters in Venezuela. He is already living that dream. Now he clearly hopes to be "someone who matters in the world." And that dream too is becoming a reality.

Chávez vs. the World

Unchecked access to a rich national treasury and the ability to spend it at his own discretion anywhere in the world have certainly helped President Chávez become an influential international figure. But his influence is not only driven by the money. It is also fed by the allure of his personal story and his irreverent, made-for-TV style. And, very important, his political message has also hit a global nerve that makes him internationally relevant.

Chávez identifies themes that have political resonance beyond Venezuela. His denunciations of corruption, economic inequality, and social exclusion have been constant fixtures of his rhetoric. He was early in detecting that these perennial themes had acquired renewed political potency in the 1990s, and he very effectively made them the pillars of his political message at home. He soon realized that his themes had strong echoes elsewhere and that political leaders in other countries who adopted them made great strides in popularly. In many countries, fighting for equality became more important than promoting prosperity, fighting corruption became a larger goal than defending democracy, and fighting social exclusion became far more important than boosting economic efficiency.

The messages that helped propel [Palestinian Islamic organization] Hamas to electoral victory in Palestine or Mahmoud Ahmadinejad in Iran, for example, bear a striking resemblance to those that Chávez had been stridently hammering for a decade. The same ideas are fueling the popularity of countless politicians in Central and Eastern Europe, parts of Asia, and all of Latin America. Of course, they differ in context and nuance; religion, for example, weighs far more heavily in local politics in the Middle East than in Latin America. But despite their differences, what these successful politicians have in common is the ability to persuade the electorate that they are better than their rivals at listening to the poor, fighting public corruption, correcting longstanding inequities, or delivering food subsidies and social services, especially health and education. Their more concrete promises are far more powerful drivers of electoral support than the allure of the larger geopolitical struggles in which these politicians are also engaged. President Ahmadinejad in Iran was elected because he was seen as the honest and competent mayor of Tehran [Iran's capital], not because Iranian voters were looking for a president who would wipe out Israel or build a nuclear bomb. Voters care more about getting a job or a cash subsidy, or ousting thieving politicians, than about the latest real or imagined threat coming from the devilish American superpower....

The Truth of Chávez's Policies

It is important to recognize that Hugo Chávez is one of the most astute politicians in power today in Latin America. In the long run his economic policies will surely hurt the material well-being of most Venezuelans, and his authoritarian behavior is clearly eroding the basic political freedoms that the country enjoyed for decades. The damages inflicted by the cult of personality, institutional devastation, and militarization of Venezuela's political life will take years to repair. But to a majority of poor Venezuelans, none of this matters. For them,

Hugo Chávez is the leader who provides what no other before him gave them: a sense that he cares deeply, almost personally, for each one of them. A large number of Venezuelans voted for Chávez not as the lesser of several evils but as their leader, one who speaks to their wants and needs. "He cares about people like me." "He represents me." "Even if my situation has not gotten better, at least I know he is trying." These are the phrases one hears in the barrios across Venezuela.

But Chávez is reinforced by his clever exploitation of the three themes that drive the political behavior of most Venezuelans: the need to wage war against corruption, inequality, and injustice.

Excessive Power in the US Executive Branch

Gene Healy

Gene Healy, journalist and vice president of the Cato Institute, has had as his special interest the abuse of executive power.

In his Afterword to a 2008 study of excessive presidential power, Healy discusses the gradual expansion of Article II of the US Constitution, which defines the executive branch of government. During George W. Bush's terms, Healy says, Congress allowed the president excessive power to wage war, to spy on citizens, and to address the financial crises. Healy also criticizes Bush's Treasury secretary for demanding unchecked authority over bailout money, likening the secretary to "the modern equivalent of a Roman dictator for economic affairs." Additionally, Healy argues that Barack Obama's campaign promises for proper limits on executive power have proved superficial; Obama has carried over Bush's policies for torture, privacy, and bailout programs. Yet Healy says it is too soon to tell whether Obama will handle the "war on terror" responsibly, and he concludes that strong presidents are those who resist the expansion of power.

The weeks after the Republican National Convention [of 2008] saw an intensification of the ongoing financial meltdown with the collapse of Lehman Brothers, the federal takeover of Fannie Mae and Freddie Mac, and the bailout of mega-insurer American International Group. [John] McCain's poll numbers, which had enjoyed a brief, post-convention bounce, fell rapidly. After his gimmicky late-September decision to suspend his campaign and push for a bank bailout, McCain's campaign never recovered.

Bush's Extraordinary Power to Deal with Economic Meltdown

George W. Bush's lame-duck period repeated the pattern that had prevailed throughout his two terms: the announcement of an unprecedented crisis, demands for new presidential powers to meet that crisis, and—after some perfunctory grumbling—Congress's capitulation to those demands.

In his seminal book *Presidential Power and the Modern Presidents*, [political scientist] Richard Neustadt argued that the presidency is an inherently weak office, and to grow its powers, the president needs to build up political capital and spend it wisely. But oddly enough, although our massively unpopular president's political capital had evaporated early in his second term, George W. Bush continued to secure broad new grants of authority from Congress. Nobody liked the president, nobody trusted him—but everybody looked to him to solve all of America's problems.

Treasury Secretary Henry Paulson's original three-page proposal for a bank bailout demanded unchecked power over some $700 billion in taxpayer assets, "Decisions by the Secretary pursuant to the authority of this Act are non-reviewable and committed to agency discretion, and may not be reviewed by any court of law or any administrative agency." That provision didn't make it into the final bill, the Emergency Economic Stabilization Act of 2008, which passed on October 3, allowing the executive branch to set up the Troubled Assets Relief Program (TARP) to purchase toxic mortgage-backed securities. Nonetheless, by the end of 2008, Paulson looked a lot like the modern equivalent of a Roman dictator for economic affairs, using a broad delegation of authority from Congress to decide which financial institutions would live and which would die.

In December 2008, American automakers General Motors [GM] and Chrysler tottered on the brink of bankruptcy, while Congress debated legislation to provide some $15 billion to keep two of the "Big Three" alive. On December 11, the auto bailout bill failed to pass a key procedural vote in the Senate. But a week later, Bush announced that, despite the bill's failure, he had decided to lend the car companies $17.4 billion. White House spokesman Tony Fratto explained:

> Congress lost its opportunity to be a partner because they couldn't get their job done.... This is not the way we wanted to deal with this issue. We wanted to deal with it in partnership. What Congress said is ... "We can't get it done, so it's up to the White House to get it done."

As the Bush administration saw it, then, by not giving the president the power to bail out the automakers, Congress "lost its opportunity to be a partner," and the president had every right to order the bailout anyway.

Administrative Lawlessness

Some commentators cited that decision as yet another example of Bush administration lawlessness. The president claimed that he had the power to act under TARP, the operative clause of which gave the secretary of the treasury the power to buy "troubled assets" from "financial institutions." The Bush administration had interpreted that authority broadly, abandoning the original plan almost immediately and using TARP to buy shares in banks—some of which, such as Wells Fargo, weren't "troubled." But using the legislation to bail out car companies seemed a bridge too far. How could a statute empowering the executive branch to buy mortgage-backed securities from banks be used to lend money to automakers, which surely couldn't qualify as "financial institutions"? Having repeatedly insisted that he could not be bound by validly enacted statutes in matters related to national security, it seemed that President Bush had decided he couldn't be bound by clear statutory language when it came to addressing the nation's economic woes.

The truth was even more disturbing. A closer look at the TARP statute reveals that Congress wrote legislative language so irresponsibly broad that the administration actually had a colorable argument that it could reshape the bailout as it saw fit.

Various members of Congress angrily protested that the president had gone from buying toxic assets to recapitalizing banks to bailing out carmakers—shifting priorities almost daily, regardless of what Congress believed it had authorized. But after ceding vast authority to the president, legislators' outrage was more than a day late and $700 billion short. Once again, on a core issue of governance, Congress had abdicated its legislative responsibilities, leaving the hard choices to the president. The buck stops *there*.

Two weeks after Bush bailed out GM and Chrysler, *Newsweek*'s cover story focused on presidential power. The lead article, by Stuart Taylor Jr. and Evan Thomas, rang the changes on an all-too familiar theme: the dangers of an enervated executive branch. "By trying to strengthen the presidency," Taylor and Thomas argued, Bush and [Vice President Dick] Cheney "weakened it." They quoted former Office of Legal Counsel head Jack Goldsmith, who maintained that we should be "less worried about an out-of-control presidency than an enfeebled one."

At a time when the Treasury secretary was busily reshaping the commanding heights of finance with precious little input from Congress, it was hard to understand how anyone could think that the executive branch had lost power during the previous eight years. But Taylor and Thomas were on to something when they argued that [President Barack] Obama might be pressured into maintaining certain aspects of the Bush approach to the War on Terror.

The conventional narrative about the Bush power grab blames Dick Cheney, David Addington, John Yoo, and the other administration figures whose ideological commitment to unchecked executive power long predated September 11 [referring to the terrorist attacks on the United States in 2001]. The conventional narrative isn't wrong; it's just incomplete. It ignores the role of public demands for presidential action, which can force presidents to seek or accept new powers they'd never previously craved. . . .

Obama Is a Bundle of Contradictions

On the campaign trail, Barack Obama signaled that, if elected, he'd take a very different approach to executive power. He'd forcefully criticized Bush's claim to be sole constitutional "decider" on all matters involving national security. And in Obama's answers to reporter Charlie Savage's December 2007 executive power questionnaire, he made it clear that he *didn't* think Article II of the Constitution gave the president unchecked power. "The President," Senator Obama wrote, "does not have power under the Constitution to unilaterally authorize a military attack in a situation that does not involve stopping an actual or imminent threat to the nation." Neither, in Obama's view, did he have the power to ignore statutes governing surveillance and treatment of enemy combatants.

As he came closer to winning the office, however, he reversed himself on national security wiretapping. When Senator Obama acquiesced to the FISA [Financial Information Services Agency] Amendments Act in summer 2008, he broke an explicit campaign promise to filibuster any legislation that would grant immunity to FISA-flouting telecom companies. And by voting for the bill, Obama helped legalize large swaths of a dragnet surveillance program he'd long claimed to oppose.

Perhaps some were comforted by Obama's "firm pledge" that "as president, I will carefully monitor the program." But our constitutional structure envisions stronger checks than the supposed benevolence of our leaders. Civil libertarians had good reason to fear that, once elected, Obama would, like other presidents, "grow in office."

And yet, in the early days of his administration, Obama seemed determined to confound the cynics. In his first full day as president, Obama halted all military commission trials. At a swearing-in ceremony for senior executive branch officials, he told the attendees, "For a long time now, there's been too much secrecy in this city." He issued a directive to "the Heads of Executive Departments and Agencies" on interpreting the Freedom of Information Act [FOIA], "All agencies should adopt a presumption in favor of disclosure, in order to renew their commitment to the principles embodied in FOIA, and to usher in a new era of open Government. The presumption of disclosure should be applied to all decisions involving FOIA."

Call it the "soft bigotry of low expectations," if you will, but it was genuinely heartening when, the next day, the new president ordered the executive branch to *obey the law*. Obama issued an executive order making it clear that the executive branch had to comply with federal statutes governing torture.

Equally important were Obama's appointments to the Office of Legal Counsel, the institution that provides legal advice to the president as to the limits of his Article II powers. The people Obama picked to set legal policy for the executive branch made for a stark contrast with the Bush administration. . . .

Obama's Use of Power

Civil libertarian euphoria faded rather quickly, however. A few weeks after the initial flurry of executive orders, in a case alleging that the Bush administration had broken the law by facilitating the torture of terrorist suspects, the Obama legal team took the same position the Bush administration had. They argued that the State Secrets Privilege didn't merely prevent the disclosure of sensitive pieces of evidence. It allowed the federal government to suppress the entire lawsuit and to send the litigants home. Shortly thereafter, Obama's lawyers took the same position in a case that challenged Bush's warrantless wiretapping program, making the administration complicit in covering up illegal activity by its predecessor. In early March [2009], the president issued his first signing statement, objecting to several provisions in a $410 billion omnibus spending bill. Reserving the right to ignore or evade one such provision—which would restrict his ability to place U.S. troops under foreign command—Obama invoked his authority under the Commander-in-Chief clause.

As of this writing [in 2009], the evidence is mixed, and it's far too early to tell whether Obama intends to meaningfully relimit executive power in the War on Terror. If he does, he deserves enormous credit. Presidential self-restraint is a rare thing, and we ought to applaud it if and when it happens. The perennial presidential ranking polls show that far too many scholars overvalue strong presidents—where "strong" is defined as aggressively expanding the powers of the office. What the presidential rankers too often miss is that it takes a strong president to *resist* maximizing his power.

For Further Discussion

1. What in William Shakespeare's life may have caused both resentment toward absolute power and wariness of it? See Andrews, Greenblatt, and Ackroyd.

2. How may English history have parallels with ancient Rome? See Greenblatt, Hadfield, Rebhorn, and Rosen.

3. Is Brutus portrayed as the hero? See Hadfield, Rosen, Gil, Miola, Fergusson, and Bulman.

4. In what sense is Caesar portrayed as a tyrant? Is his murder justified? See Hadfield, Gil, Miola, and Bulman.

5. To what extent does the play show that revolution is inevitably disruptive and harmful? See Rosen and Fergusson.

6. Critics argue over whether Caesar is admirable or a tyrant. To what extent are current world leaders seen as ambiguous—both intolerant of challenges to their power and courageous reformers? See Naji, Erikson, and Naím.

For Further Reading

Plutarch, "The Life of Julius Caesar." In *Lives of the Noble Grecians and Romans*. Ed. Paul Turner. Carbondale: Southern Illinois University Press, 1963.

————, "The Life of Brutus." In *Lives of the Noble Grecians and Romans*. Ed. Paul Turner. Carbondale: Southern Illinois University Press, 1963.

William Shakespeare, *The Tragedy of Antony and Cleopatra*. In *The Riverside Shakespeare*. Ed. G. Blakemore Evans. Boston: Houghton Mifflin, 1974.

————, *The Tragedy of Coriolanus*. In *The Riverside Shakespeare*. Ed. G. Blakemore Evans. Boston: Houghton Mifflin, 1974.

————, *The Tragedy of Macbeth*. In *The Riverside Shakespeare*. Ed. G. Blakemore Evans. Boston: Houghton Mifflin, 1974.

————, *The Tragedy of King Richard II*. In *The Riverside Shakespeare*. Ed. G. Blakemore Evans. Boston: Houghton Mifflin, 1974.

————, *The Tragedy of Richard the Third*. In *The Riverside Shakespeare*. Ed. G. Blakemore Evans. Boston: Houghton Mifflin, 1974.

————, *The First Part of Henry IV*. In *The Riverside Shakespeare*. Ed. G. Blakemore Evans. Boston: Houghton Mifflin, 1974.

————, *The Second Part of Henry IV*. In *The Riverside Shakespeare*. Ed. G. Blakemore Evans. Boston: Houghton Mifflin, 1974.

————, *The Life of Henry the Fifth*. In *The Riverside Shakespeare*. Ed. G. Blakemore Evans. Boston: Houghton Mifflin, 1974.

Bibliography

Books

Ann Louise
Bardach

*Cuba Confidential: Love and
Vengeance in Miami and Havana.*
New York: Random House, 2002.

Adrien Bonjour

The Structure of Julius Caesar.
Liverpool: Liverpool University Press,
1958.

Fredson Bowers

*Elizabethan Revenge Tragedy,
1587-1642.* Princeton: Princeton
University Press, 1940.

Martin Bradley

*Under the Loving Care of the Fatherly
Leader: North Korea and the Kim
Family.* New York: Thomas Dunne
Books, 2004.

Reuben A. Brower

*Hero and Saint: Shakespeare and the
Graeco-Roman Heroic Tradition.* New
York: Oxford University Press, 1971.

Paul A. Cantor

*Shakespeare's Rome, Republic and
Empire.* Ithaca, NY: Cornell
University Press, 1976.

Feliks Gross

The Seizure of Political Power. New
York: Philosophical Library, 1958.

A.D. Nuttall

Shakespeare the Thinker. New Haven,
CT: Yale University Press, 2007.

A.L. Rowse

William Shakespeare: A Biography.
New York: Harper & Row, 1963.

Samuel
Schoenbaum

William Shakespeare: A Documentary Life. New York: Oxford University Press, 1975.

Joseph Larry
Simmons

Shakespeare's Pagan World: The Roman Tragedies. Charlottesville: University Press of Virginia, 1973.

Ronald Syme

The Roman Revolution. Oxford: Oxford University Press, 2002.

Periodicals

John Alvis

"The Coherence of Shakespeare's Roman Plays," *Modern Language Quarterly*, vol. 40, 1979.

Barbara J. Bono

"The Birth of Tragedy: Tragic Action of *Julius Caesar*," *English Literary Renaissance*, vol. 24, no. 2, Spring 1994.

D.S. Brewer

"Brutus's Crime: A Footnote to *Julius Caesar*," *Review of English Studies*, vol. III, no. 9, January 1952.

John Drakakis

"'Fashion It Thus,' *Julius Caesar* and the Politics of Theatrical Representation," *Shakespeare Survey*, vol. 44, 1992.

Celia W. Dugger

"Party Leaders Say Mugabe Will Fight On," *New York Times*, April 5, 2008.

Nader Hashemi

"The Battle for Iran," *Nation*, vol. 290, no. 4, February 1, 2010.

Nat Hentoff   "Roar, Tyrants, You Cannot Hide Your Racist Deeds," *Zanesville Times-Recorder*, January 9, 2010.

Richard Hosley   "The Discovery-Space in Shakespeare's Globe," *Shakespeare Survey*, vol. 12, 1959.

L.C. Knights   "Shakespeare and Political Wisdom: A Note on the Personalism of *Julius Caesar* and *Coriolanus*," *Sewanee Review*, vol. 61, no. 1, Winter 1953.

D.J. Palmer   "Tragic Error in *Julius Caesar*," *Shakespeare Quarterly*, vol. 21, no. 4, Autumn 1970.

Barbara L. Parker   "'A Thing Unfirm': Plato's *Republic* and *Julius Caesar*," *Shakespeare Quarterly*, vol. 44, no. 1, Spring 1993.

Mark Rose   "Conjuring Caesar: Ceremony, History, and Authority in 1599," *English Literary Renaissance*, vol. 19, no. 3, December 1989.

Tavia Tyong'o   "Kenya's Crisis," *Nation*, January 28, 2008.

John W. Velz   "Orator and Imperator in *Julius Caesar*: Style and the Process of Roman History," *Shakespeare Studies*, vol. 15, 1982.

Internet Sources

Scott Horton — "More Evidence of an Emerging Military Dictatorship in Iran," *Harper's Magazine*, November 30, 2009. www.harpers.org.

Takavafira Zhou — "They Made Me Chant Robert Mugabe Is Always Right, While I Was Being Beaten," *Independent*, March 8, 2008. www.independent.co.uk.

Index